Optimists
ALWAYS
Win!

Optimists ALWAYS *Win!*

Moving from Defeat to Life's C-Suite

Kimberly S. Reed, MEd

Foreword by Dahlia M. Sataloff, MD, FACS

Health Communications, Inc.
Deerfield Beach, Florida

www.hcibooks.com

Library of Congress Control Number: 2020948194

ISBN-13: 978-07573-2105-4 (Paperback)
ISBN-10: 07573-2105-4 (Paperback)
ISBN-13: 978-07573-2357-7 (ePub)
ISBN-10: 07573-2357-X (ePub)

Publisher: Health Communications, Inc.
        1700 NW 2nd Avenue
        Boca Raton, FL 33432-1653

Cover design by Lawna Patterson Oldfield
Interior design by Larissa Hise Henoch, formatting by Lawna Patterson Oldfield

In loving memory of
Grandmother Mary J. Morris
Beloved mother and soror, Barbara E. Reed
Grandmother Hattie V. Reed
To every courageous warrior and survivor who never
stops fighting and believing there is a champion in YOU!
To all the amazing and caring doctors and nurses at Penn
Medicine's Abramson Cancer Center and Hartford Hospital

CONTENTS

FOREWORD

LIFE IS FULL OF THE UNEXPECTED. There are choices to be made that can significantly alter the direction and fulfillment of one's life. We are all faced with wonderful opportunities, but also with adversity, which can sometimes be devastating and even life-threatening. The good times in life are generally easier to navigate–hope, opportunity, and success are great things to anticipate. Yet, it is often how we deal with adversity that tests our strength and defines us. Faced with seemingly insurmountable odds, some of us choose pessimism and defeat, while others refuse to accept defeat and strive forward with optimism and determination.

None of us will navigate through life without some sort of medical issue, often serious. Cancer is unfortunately common, and virtually all of us either know someone battling the disease, or we may even have faced it personally. We all strive to find the best medical providers at the best institutions for treatment. However, our approach to these issues also can have significant effects on the outcome. Having a positive outlook, optimism, and strength are critical.

Kimberly S. Reed's life was turned upside-down with the sudden death of her beloved mother and her grandmother. She was dealing with these tragic life events when she herself was diagnosed with breast cancer. Initially, the cancer was thought to be localized, but subsequently it was determined to have spread—Stage IV. An aggressive, personalized treatment plan was devised including major surgeries, chemotherapy, targeted therapy, and radiation.

Faced with this daunting diagnosis and difficult treatments, Kim never wavered, never complained or asked "why me," and never lost faith. She maintained an unshakably positive attitude, determined to beat the odds and declare victory over this dreaded disease. She recovered from her treatment and has been cancer-free for over five years following her diagnosis.

I had the privilege of being one of Kim's doctors and was with her throughout the treatment process, and I continue to monitor her breast health. Her optimistic, determined attitude and approach to adversity are inspiring. As is typical of Kim, she wanted to share her journey, with the hope of helping others facing similar adversity. She wanted to highlight the power of an optimistic attitude and elimination of negativity to emerge victorious.

Kim is a motivational speaker. She reaches a large audience with her words of encouragement and guidance to a better, more fulfilling life. But that wasn't enough for Kim. She decided to write a book outlining steps to eliminate discouragement and reach the pinnacle in life. The message of *Optimists Always Win! Moving from Defeat to Life's C-Suite* is simple: difficulties and struggles are unavoidable in life, but every one of us has complete control of his or her personal response to adversity. Responding with optimism and hope in difficult circumstances is not easy. This book provides concrete steps to help us counteract negativity and pessimism; learn from the pastbut focus on the future; and strive forward with hope and promise.

There are other books that address similar concepts, but few are as inspiring and motivating as this one. Kim gives the reader ten concrete tools to eliminate discouragement and embrace an optimistic attitude to apply to his or her own battles, to succeed in overcoming adversity. This book is a must-read for everyone facing life's difficult challenges—which means all of us at some point in our lives. Kim helps us regard challenges not as tragedies, but rather as opportunities to become the best we can be.

—Dahlia M. Sataloff, MD
Professor of Clinical Surgery, Perelman School
of Medicine at the University of Pennsylvania
Chair, Department of Surgery, Pennsylvania Hospital

A NOTE FROM THE AUTHOR

AT SOME POINT IN LIFE, we all eventually face something much bigger than we are. We all get in situations—some by fate, others by our own doing—that seem too big to overcome. I call these life knockouts (LKOs). If you have ever experienced an LKO or are in the midst of one, this book is for you. If life seems to be knocking you down with little hits more often than it lifts you up, this book is also for you.

In boxing, a referee declares a technical knockout (TKO) if they determine that a fighter cannot safely continue the match for any reason. There's no need for an intervening count. Similarly, a life knockout (LKO) is a life circumstance that renders a person mentally, physically, spiritually, or emotionally incapable of continuing life in their usual manner. A person experiencing an LKO is so impaired by the current crisis or challenge that they are unable to see any possibility for a positive or victorious outcome. That person is figuratively "down for the count." But that is precisely when they need to keep fighting.

People often fixate on the negative side of life, perpetually seeing the figurative glass as half empty, dwelling on insults, and focusing on mistakes. This is because our brain's default setting is to give greater weight to the negative things that happen to us than to the positive things. Psychologists refer to this as the negativity bias. And, unfortunately, it is an inherent trait of most humans. Ask anyone who has ever tried to lose weight, develop a new skill, or incorporate a new habit, for example. They can tell you from firsthand experience that focusing on the difficulty of the task rather than on the positivity of achievement is our natural tendency. The good news is that developing optimism can overpower our inherent inclination to focus on the negative side of challenges and pitfalls.

Optimists Always Win is designed to help you develop a process to stay optimistic at all times. To be clear, being optimistic does not mean that you are always happy or that sugar will fall from the sky. Choosing to be optimistic acknowledges that we have the ability to positively interpret the meaning of our life events, or as Tony Robbins puts it: "It's not the events of our lives that shape us, but our beliefs as to what those events mean." Optimism is the most salient trait we have because it allows us to evolve our thought process, better our situation, and put our faith and hope in a better tomorrow.

While I've always made an effort to be optimistic, there were times in my life when I was enormously challenged by circumstances. Truthfully, some moments would make me feel more like a hypocrite than an optimistic warrior, but I held on. After successfully beating cancer years earlier, my mom lost her battle forty-five short days after her second diagnosis. She had been my "shero," my confidant, my very best friend, and an integral part of my heart and soul. Her death caused me to fall harder than I had ever fallen before. That was a huge LKO. Additionally, just as I was beginning the grieving process, I learned that I had breast cancer. Another LKO. But instead of going down for the count, I needed to gear up for the literal fight of my life and get back in the ring! I was determined to regain my balance and come back more victorious than ever. But how? Determination? Resilience? Courage? Faith? Optimism?

When you are running on empty, how do you face LKOs? After experiencing my own LKOs, I can make a solid argument—backed up by tears, isolation, fear, and hitting emotional rock bottom—that in the face of extreme adversity, optimism is the soul's rocket fuel. Optimism *will* give you the strength to deal with all your setbacks and hardships.

I have lived by the principles in this book; they are etched in my DNA. Yes, they were challenged by the LKOs I faced, and I had to recommit to them. In doing so, I have seen the many benefits of optimism manifest in my life. Once you have finished reading this book, my prayer is that you, too, will enjoy the benefits of taking a more optimistic approach to life as well as to any LKOs that might knock you down.

Hold my hand and walk with me,

Kim, LKO Survivor

INTRODUCTION

EVEN IF YOU AREN'T A FAN of superheroes, you probably know that Superman uses his extraordinary abilities to benefit humanity and that kryptonite negates his invincibility and can even incapacitate him. When the kryptonite is removed, Superman quickly rejuvenates. While we aren't superheroes, we have all been created to fulfill a unique purpose in the world to benefit humanity, and, like Superman, we are all susceptible to some form of "kryptonite"—for example, a loss of faith, a dismal outlook for the future, toxic people and relationships, worry, and regrets. All of these things discourage us from being optimistic.

At some point in life, everyone must deal with challenges only they can fight. The key is knowing how to respond to situations and circumstances and being able to rejuvenate quickly once the "kryptonite" is removed. If someone focuses only on the negative, they are missing out on potential positive outcomes. What's more, dwelling on negativity results in even more negativity, making it much more difficult to access optimism. A negative outlook restricts our future and potential to succeed to the degree that we completely miss the blessings intended for us.

Switching from negativity to an optimistic viewpoint is a choice everyone can make. It starts with a shift in focus and increases from there. The 2017 Super Bowl is an excellent example of this.

The Patriots were down 28 to 3, but Tom Brady still believed his team could win. His optimism spread throughout the team, and they had the greatest comeback in a title game of any team across any major sport. Without Brady's optimistic confidence, the Patriots might have had a very different outcome. Brady realized something I learned long ago—that optimists always win! It may not translate to a perfect season, winning the title every year, closing every contract desired, having a great date every time you go out, and so on. But what it does mean is that you know that every day is a fresh start, which positively influences your behavior and effectiveness moving forward.

You do *not* have to face adversity with pessimism or hopelessness. There is a better way, though it may at first seem counterintuitive. Relying heavily on the optimism I tapped into during my crises, I developed ten "discouragement eliminators," which I share with you in this book. These eliminators not only helped me navigate my tremendous grief and succeed in my fight against cancer but also changed how I live each day as my best self.

The National Cancer Institute estimates that roughly 1.8 million people will be diagnosed with cancer in the United States in 2020, so the odds of knowing someone who is affected by this disease are high. Hopefully, you and your loved ones will avoid this dreaded disease, but the one thing that no one can avoid in this life are trials and tribulations. Eventually, they darken all our doorsteps. My goal in this book is simple: to teach you how to take complete control of how you respond to difficulties and struggles in your life. Responding with optimism to both the challenges and blessings is often easier said than done, but it *is* possible. I know because I've endured adversities and devastating difficulties with optimism.

The Trials of Kim

My aunt, who was one of my mother's best friends, lost her battle with multiple myeloma in 2009. Both she and my mom were battling their cancers at the same time, but my mother defeated hers. Three years later, however, my mom's cancer returned, and this time the illness claimed her life, on July 31, 2012. Three months after my mom's death, my eighty-eight-year-old grandmother fell ill. I believe her heartbroken state over the loss of her two daughters made her too weak to fight against the sickness that would claim her life.

Days before I joined my family to bury my grandmother, I learned that my mammogram result was abnormal. Soon after, further tests indicated that I, too, was now battling the dreaded disease—breast cancer. I managed to get through the funeral without sharing my news. I kept this secret from my family, especially my father. I could not bear the thought of his thinking that he was destined to be alone on this earth after losing his beloved wife of forty-four years. A few days before I started chemotherapy, I did tell my dad just in case anything adverse happened during my treatment sessions.

Like the biblical character Job, who suffered a series of tragedies after years of living a picture-perfect life, I experienced hit after hit, and just when I thought I was managing life and fighting back against the disease attacking my body, I received one more blow. A spot on my liver required me to undergo surgery. However, my story turned out the same way Job's did. Job rose victorious and received double the blessings from God after making the correct choice—to trust God and His outcome instead of listening to the naysayers in his life, and so did mine! I came out stronger and with more faith than before the trial began. Three surgeries and the ordeal of chemo treatment behind me, I can shout my war cry,

"I'm cancer-free!" Now, I share how my faith was strengthened through my mother's salient example, my real-life hero. I also practice what I preach by living a life of optimism, even amid my personal battles. If you or anyone you know is struggling to win a battle in health or just with difficulty in life, my story can inspire you to live in such a way that counteracts the negative thinking of the world.

We all face trials in life and sometimes get into in situations that seem too big to overcome. Even in the face of such trying circumstances, the ten discouragement eliminators in this book will help you obtain a level of happiness, peace, wisdom, and growth in all areas of your life—what I call the "C-suite," which you'll learn more about later in the book. For now, just know that achieving C-suite living is choosing optimism over anger, bitterness, negativity, and/or revenge.

In his books and articles, bestselling author Harvey Mackay acknowledges the power of optimism. He reiterates the sentiment that "A pessimist sees the difficulty in every opportunity; an optimist sees the opportunity in every difficulty." While positive thinking alone may not ensure success, it does help us persevere against the setbacks that we encounters throughout life. In a May 2017 article on his website, Mackay writes, "How you look at life can drastically affect how much you enjoy your life. Optimists expect the best out of life...it's an attitude that can be learned." He goes on to say, "Optimists and pessimists are both right about the same number of times, but optimists get to enjoy their lives more." With such insight, why waste time worrying? An optimistic attitude helps us enjoy life despite negative circumstances and can even help create the good outcomes we optimists expect.

What's more, being optimistic isn't just about enjoying life; it's also about feeling good. According to a March 2017 *New York Times* article "A Positive Outlook May Be Good for Your Health" by Jane E. Brody, there is a definite link between what happens in the brain and subsequently what happens in the body. For example, when facing a crisis of illness, choosing optimism "can boost the immune system and counter depression." An optimistic attitude has been shown to have health benefits such as reduced risk of heart disease, better weight control, lower blood pressure, and healthier blood sugar levels. Even when faced with a disease such as cancer, an optimistic attitude can "improve one's quality of life."

As the *New York Times* article states, one such example is Dr. Wendy Schlessel Harpham, author and practicing internist who fought non-Hodgkin's lymphoma for fifteen years, including eight relapses. She chose to live with an optimistic attitude, and "her cancer has been in remission now for twelve years [as of 2017]." I can certainly relate. While I did experience overwhelming feelings of loss, I did not give in to feelings of hopelessness. I followed my mom's, grandmother's, and aunt's extraordinary examples of faith and gleaned wisdom from how they walked through their stories to conquer my own health battle. Though their stories did not end the way mine did, their courage and faith that life would unfold as it was meant to gave me the strength and hope I needed to remain optimistic.

As the article cited explained, "New research is demonstrating that people can learn skills that help them experience more positive emotions when faced with the severe stress of a life-threatening illness." So even if you are feeling anything but optimistic, you can still learn the skills you need to turn that around. In fact, that is the purpose of this book. The ten strategies outlined in the upcoming chapters will help you eliminate discouragement, grow in faith, and engage an optimistic attitude toward every battle you face. Using these eliminators during times of loss and while navigating my health challenges led me to experience ultimate victory after suffering the worst trials of my life. I believe these principles will do the same for you.

Before we jump into Chapter 1, complete the following assessment so you will know how you can use this book most effectively.

Self-Assessment: How Optimistic Are You?

1. At a social gathering, you see your close friend and their significant other off in a corner quietly arguing about something. You immediately think:
  a) I hope they can still enjoy the party.
  b) Whatever it is, they will work it out because they love each other.
  c) Oh no, they are breaking up!

2. You invite six close friends to your home for an intimate dinner party. The conversation is great and everyone seemed happy, but afterward, while you are storing the leftovers, you notice there is a lot more left over than you expected. You think:
  a) They didn't enjoy my cooking.
  b) I love leftovers!
  c) I made too much food.

3. Your beloved cat crosses the rainbow bridge. You think:
  a) I am so happy for the time I got to spend with fluffy. I will eventually get another cat and shower all my love on them.
  b) Why did this have to happen? Why did *my* cat have to die?
  c) I am overwhelmed with grief, and I'm not sure if I ever want another pet.

4. Your friends recently tried a new restaurant, and even though they didn't have a good experience, they invite you to go with them to give it another try. Your response is:

    a) If you guys didn't like it, I probably won't either. I'll pass.

    b) Well, I guess I can try it.

    c) Ooh, a food adventure! Sure, I'll go!

5. You are in the superstore, and someone isn't looking where they are going. They ram their shopping cart into your foot, but they apologize quickly. Your response is:

    a) Shout at the offender to watch where they're going. That *really* hurt.

    b) Shrug at them and limp away without comment.

    c) Accept their apology and make a joke about how you don't need that foot anyway.

6. You need to be at an appointment by 3:30 PM, but you are stuck in traffic. After you call to say that you will be late, what do you do?

    a) Take a deep breath and try to remain calm.

    b) Turn up the radio and enjoy a little forced downtime.

    c) Stress over the traffic and get down on yourself for not leaving earlier.

7. You are relocating to another city to be closer to a loved one and need to find a new job. How do you think your job hunt will go?

    a) I'm qualified for a number of positions, so I don't think I'll have much trouble finding something.

    b) It's going to be tough, but I suppose I'll eventually find something.

    c) I'm going to land my dream job—or something very much like it.

8. You are about to walk into an important meeting at your company. What's on your mind?

    a) I really don't belong at this meeting. I'm not sure why I was expected to attend.

b) This is my chance to share my new idea.

c) I hope this meeting is productive.

9. Your doctor's office leaves a message on your voicemail telling you that the results of your test are in and to please call back. You immediately think:

a) I won't assume it's bad news or good news before I hear the results.

b) It's bad news.

c) Whatever it is, knowing the results will bring me a step closer to good health.

10. You want to get on the list to adopt a puppy from the shelter, so you fill out all the paperwork. A couple of days pass, but you haven't heard if you are approved. You think:

a) They didn't approve me. There must be something wrong with me if they won't let me adopt a puppy.

b) My application must have gotten lost.

c) I know I'll make a great dog owner. They must be very busy.

SCORING

1	A = 10	B = 15	C = 5
2	A = 5	B = 10	C = 5
3	A = 15	B = 10	C = 5
4	A = 5	B = 10	C = 15
5	A = 5	B = 10	C = 15
6	A = 10	B = 15	C = 5
7	A = 10	B = 5	C = 15
8	A = 5	B = 15	C = 10
9	A = 10	B = 5	C = 15
10	A = 5	B = 10	C = 15

Score = 125 to 150

You're a positive person! You want to get the most out of life and enjoy making fun memories with friends and family. You have learned how to adjust to the lemons of life by making lemonade, lemon cake, and lemon pies! You can use this book to elevate the optimism you already subscribe to and use it to teach others that no matter the situation, optimists always win!

Score = 95 to 120

You're a realist. You are someone who tends to view or present things as they are at this moment. You typically think, That's just the way it is. *You usually do not dwell on the past or worry about future. You typically work and live in the moment, focusing on what is currently at hand. You can use this book to brighten your outlook and take action to make life better wherever you can.*

Score = 50 to 90

You tend to sway toward negativity. Maybe you had a rough childhood or grew up around a lot of negative people. You typically view circumstances as if the glass is half empty. One big challenge with your present view is that you could morph over time from a pessimist to a fatalist. Pessimists are usually doubtful or skeptical, but fatalists see the very worst in every situation. They always seem angry and contentious and typically pick fights. You can use this book to avoid developing a fatalist outlook and turn your pessimism around by adopting a new outlook and perspective. Share your journey with those closest to you if you struggle with being positive; ask them to hold you accountable for achieving a positive perspective.

Now that you know approximately where you fall on the optimism-pessimism spectrum, you are ready to learn how to adopt a more optimistic attitude, no matter your circumstances in life.

Each chapter focuses on eliminating a factor that can dampen or even eradicate your optimism. You'll read more about my experiences to help bring the "discouragement eliminator" more to life. Each chapter includes exercises for self-reflection, so be sure to have a pen and paper handy as you work through this book. You might even want to get a journal or notebook solely dedicated to your more optimistic lifestyle. By the time you complete the last chapter, you should be feeling happier, healthier, and more empowered!

Chapter 1

DISCOURAGEMENT ELIMINATOR 1:
Embrace a Kryptonite-Free *Life*

WE WERE EACH CREATED to fulfill a unique purpose, defeat our giants, and be modern-day heroes with a vital part to play in the world. One of the destructive elements that can prevent us from reaching our given destinies is "kryptonite." You are probably familiar with kryptonite as the meteorite from the planet Krypton that weakens Superman but is generally harmless to humans. In the same way, we each have our own form of "kryptonite" that can weaken us and diminish our superpowers, even though it may not have a detrimental effect on others.

To embrace a life of positivity and optimism, you need to know what your kryptonite is—and then avoid it. We'll look at several forms of kryptonite in this chapter so that you can take steps to eliminate its detrimental effects on your outlook.

Are People Your Kryptonite?

In a July 24, 2012, *Business Insider* article, Aimee Groth says, "When it comes to relationships, we are greatly influenced—whether we like it or not—by those closest to us. It affects our way of thinking, our self-esteem, and our decisions." In this article, she quotes motivational speaker Jim Rohn, who said, "You're the average of the five people you spend most of your time with." Here's the takeaway: If the relationships in your life are filled with drama and constantly leave you feeling drained and/or empty, it is time to make some changes to stop weakening your power. Unhealthy relationships are kryptonite to your life, your mission, and your overall goals.

If you don't water a plant it will not bloom, and the same is true for relationships. If you do not nurture your relationships, they die. However, the irony is that givers often attract takers. Some of my romantic relationships have been takers. At one point in my life, I took a good look in the mirror and asked God and myself, "What is it about me that attracts takers?" And then I did the work required to set boundaries for my future relationships.

You must establish healthy boundaries that contribute to healthy relationships. There are many resources you can turn to for learning how to set boundaries, but here are some general guidelines:

1. Spend some time thinking about your boundaries. Get clear on behaviors that you will not tolerate in your relationships.

2. Set an example of how you want to be treated by others by treating them the same way.

3. Be clear and straightforward but kind when you communicate your boundaries to others.

4. Explain why it is important and what the consequences are if your boundaries are crossed.

5. Whatever the consequence, you need to see it through if your boundary is crossed. If you let something slide, you are setting a precedent for future slip-ups.

It is extremely important to pay attention to who we are with when we feel our best. We often know when people in our lives no longer deserve VIP seating, but still we are unwilling to banish them from our building. For example, your kryptonite might be a romantic relationship you have held on to well past its expiration date because you don't want to be alone. Or it might be a former partner who left your life a long time ago that you just cannot shake because you haven't taken steps to heal from that relationship. When you don't heal, you bleed on people who did not cut you, which can cause collateral damage in their life that they don't deserve.

Perhaps it is your own flesh and blood that is weakening your power. I know you cannot necessarily banish your relatives from your life, but you *can* limit your interactions with them, especially if you do not feel your best when they are around. However, when it comes to the "family we choose"—our friends and romantic partners—we must be sure that they aren't sucking the life out of us! You must set healthy boundaries and limits so that the kryptonite nature of others does not drain you and keep you from fulfilling your purpose in life.

Writing prompt: While this topic is fresh in your mind, write about the most negative relationship in your life right now. This can be any relationship: work, family, significant other, or friend. What makes that relationship negative? Do you need to set some boundaries? Do you need to plan time away from that person? Do you need to "water" the relationship a little more? As you write, try to figure out what you can do to eliminate the effects of "people kryptonite."

Are *You* Your Kryptonite?

When you are looking to make changes in your life, sometimes you have to start with the person in the mirror (à la Michael Jackson's "Man in the Mirror"). Sometimes the worst enemy is the "inner me."

I faced the worst period of my life after the passing of the matriarchs in my family. I did not want to pray, and I did not want to hope for the best, so I shut down for a while. Have you ever written or said, "Dear God," and just stopped? I have. However, in quieting my soul, I have learned that God still hears our prayers in moments like that. I finally snapped out of my despair by drawing on my optimism, but I learned something during those "pity-party" moments. I had almost allowed fear, self-doubt, and self-sabotage to ruin my life. I was also trapped in a people-pleasing cycle and trying to recover from the residue of past dead-end relationships.

You may be able to relate. Sometimes the "wrong" people enter our lives because we do not work hard enough to become the best version of ourselves that attracts the right people. Good things will come *to* us when good things come *from* us. We attract what we are. Sometimes, our inability to say no keeps us in a cycle of turbulence and dysfunction. If we are going to break free from these destructive patterns, we must get to know ourselves and do the work necessary to evolve into the person we were destined to be. We cannot do this if we won't face our own limitations, bad habits, and insufficiencies and embrace all aspects of who we are.

The key to happiness is never, ever to lower your expectation so you won't be disappointed, but to raise your expectations to have the power, presence, faith, and life you deserve! You can have everything you desire, but you have to give it EVERY SINGLE THING you have—which includes the best version of you that you can be.

Consider having a personal conversation with one of your closest friends about your fears—things that hold you back from being the person you aspire to be. Ask for their advice about how to overcome your fears. Write their feedback on a piece of paper or in your journal. Take any action that feels right to you, but do take action.

Is Perfection Your Kryptonite?

I found my favorite definition of "perfectionist" on the *Psychology Today* website. It reads: "Perfectionism is a trait that makes life an endless report card on accomplishments or looks." Imagine the damaging effects of this type of kryptonite on your outlook if you are constantly grading yourself with Bs, Cs, Ds, and even Fs.

Perfection is an illusion, but that doesn't stop us from trying. However, if the pursuit for perfection is not used as a positive catalyst, it becomes toxic and causes us to avoid failure at all costs when, in reality, failures often lead to some of our greatest achievements. What makes extreme perfectionism so toxic is that while those in its grip desire success, they are mostly focused on avoiding failure, which results in a negative orientation. They don't believe they are loved unconditionally, expecting other people's affection and approval to be dependent on their flawless performance.

The key to negating this type of kryptonite is to understand that failure is not an end; it is a lesson that opens the doors to new possibilities. In fact, it is often the beginning of something great. When things are good, we coast along without making any quantum leaps. When things go wrong, our world gets shaken up, which requires us to grow, see new things, and start fresh. An optimistic attitude allows us to learn from failures, pick up the pieces, and move on to something greater.

We cannot afford to be so consumed by perfection that we attempt to skip the process of becoming great. One of the many things I learned during the COVID-19 pandemic is that every challenging moment in my life brings an opportunity to learn something that contributes to our greatness. Many counted out 2020, but I counted it in because, during this time, our growth has been constant. The pandemic has challenged me to save money, be more creative and innovative with my business and clients, and level up my virtual-training skills; it exposed a few people in my life for who I knew they were; and I became better connected with family and friends because I had better time management. I also purged, reorganized, and enjoyed my "me time," always flowing with the upside of life. Perfection has nothing to do with it.

Is Regret Your Kryptonite?

Some of the most potent kryptonite comes in the form of regrets. When we dwell on the past, bemoaning what happened and how it *should* have gone, we spiral into a sea of negativity that ultimately restricts our potential to succeed; we may completely miss the blessings life has in store for us and even those already bestowed upon us.

I spent time in two dead-end relationships. In each case, I hoped the relationship would lead to marriage, but I ended up wasting time and energy trying to make it work. I could have spent a lifetime regretting that I did not make better choices, but I know that the lessons I learned and the experiences I had made me the woman I am today.

We cannot go back in time and change a second, no matter how much attention we put there. There is just no upside to being prisoners to our past. Living with constant, nagging regret is kryptonite for the future. The only thing it does is rob us of the present opportunities to make the most of the moments we still have.

We can let go of regret by practicing forgiveness (for ourselves and others), self-love, and healing, and recognizing that the present moment is truly a gift. It behooves us to treasure each day we have.

Is Worry Your Kryptonite?

Worry is the flip side of regret. Worry about what's to come is akin to living in the future, in which case, we are once again missing out on the present. Worry can take the form of anxiety or manifest as trying to control the future through tedious, rigid planning. This form of kryptonite reminds me of scriptures my grandmother used to read when I was younger. These words of wisdom, which can help negate this form of kryptonite, are found in Matthew 6:25–34:

25 *"That is why I tell you not to worry about everyday life—whether you have enough food and drink, or enough clothes to wear. Isn't life more than food, and your body more than clothing?* **26** *Look at the birds. They don't plant or harvest or store food in barns, for your heavenly Father feeds them. And aren't you far more valuable to him than they are?* **27** *Can all your worries add a single moment to your life?*

28 *"And why worry about your clothing? Look at the lilies of the field and how they grow. They don't work or make their clothing.* **29** *Yet Solomon in all his glory was not dressed as beautifully as they are.* **30** *And if God cares so wonderfully for wildflowers that are here today and thrown into the fire tomorrow, he will certainly care for you. Why do you have so little faith?* **34** *So don't worry about tomorrow, for tomorrow will bring its own worries. Today's trouble is enough for today.*

Verse 27 asks, "Can all your worries add a single moment to your life?" No matter our faith and whether or not we follow Scripture, worrying about what's going to happen (or what might have already happened) cannot add a minute, hour, or day to our life. In reality, the opposite is true: worry and anxiety steal away moments of joy and peace.

Living a Kryptonite-Free Life

Many psychologists classify the population as predominantly optimistic—some claiming 80 percent of people are optimistic, others stating that 60 percent of us are *somewhat* optimistic. This seems an optimistic appraisal to me. Some experts believe that optimism itself may affect the validity of research on positivity. What I know for sure is that once you eliminate the kryptonite from your life, you can truly begin experiencing a paradigm shift toward perpetual optimism. Research shows that optimism is correlated with increased life expectancy; better health; increased success in academia, work, and sports; and higher chances of recovery from adversity.

Does thinking positively make us healthier? Or is it that being healthier *leads us* to think positively? Optimism is a broad personality trait—it makes us believe that good things will be plentiful in the future and bad ones scarce. But can people who weren't born on the "right" side learn to be more optimistic? This simple question creates many discrepancies. Some researchers believe we can learn to be more optimistic, while others think we simply learn to reduce our pessimism. Either way, we will be less inclined toward negative thinking.

Positive thinking encourages us to take risks and expand our horizons. But if not appropriately weighed, it can also lead us to ignore life's dangers or exaggerate our own capabilities. There is a difference between blind faith and choosing to see the glass half full. We still must weigh decisions in our lives appropriately. We must not make choices without researching the pros and cons. We cannot afford to roll the dice on critical life issues and just wish for the best. That is not what I mean by being optimistic. As positive psychologist Suzanne C. Segerstrom, author of *Breaking Murphy's Law,* said, "Optimists are happy and healthy not because of who they are but because of how they act." I encourage you to align your actions with your positive thinking and embrace a kryptonite-free life. You will be amazed by the difference it makes.

My Memory Vault

Each night for the past seven years, before I turn off the lights and fall asleep, I recall one of my best memories of spending time with my mom. I started this routine *not* because I felt like I needed to be more positive (I already considered myself an optimist) but because I wanted to remember what mattered to me—even if those things seemed small. Now I have an overflow of amazing memories in my memory vault. This is a running reminder of all the things I appreciate in my life, things I shared with my mom, the laughs we had, and her lessons on how to live with joy.

When I first committed to this routine, I established some ground rules. The first rule, and most obvious, is that I have to think of a memory every day. The next rule is that I can't start thinking about the memories until right before bed when my mind is quiet. The third rule is to limit myself to *one* awesome memory (not simply list all the great things that come into my head all at once). Some days this task is easy, and other days it is extremely diffi-cult, but the process itself has been invaluable. I encourage you to begin your own memory vault as you set out on your journey toward a more optimistic life.

Exercise: Envision Your Best Possible Self

Go someplace where you can be alone. Have your journal or notebook handy. Get comfortable and close your eyes. Ask yourself, "What does the ideal version of me look like?"

Imagine that you have managed to realize all your life goals and you have lived up to your best possible potential. You feel satisfied with who you are and the circumstances of your life. Be as specific as possible and really see yourself as the best possible version you can imagine, personally and professionally. (The laws of nature still count so avoid creating a superhuman image!)

Once you've spent some time with this visualization, describe your best possible self in your journal in story format.

Now, list all of the goals this version of you has accomplished.

Next, think of present actions you can take to move your life in the direction of your best possible self. What skills do you need? What can you do to acquire those skills? Write these actions down, and let them direct the decisions you make in the present.

Revisit this vision of your best possible self as well as all the notes you've made for the next 21 days.

Chapter 2

● ●

DISCOURAGEMENT ELIMINATOR 2:
Define Your Life's *C-Suite*

C-SUITE IS A TERM used to refer a corporation's most important senior executives—the people who basically run the show. Do you know who's running the show of you? When you define your life's C-suite and get those high-level offices filled with only the best, you know that who you are is being run by your best, most high-level qualities. But before we can fully explore which qualities make up your C-suite, we need to get a little clearer on what optimism is. Some foundational information is necessary before you can unlock your life's C-suite team.

A Deeper Dive into Optimism

Optimism comes from the Latin word *optimus*, meaning "best." An optimistic person is always looking for the best in any situation and expecting good things to happen. Even if something negative happens, such as the loss of a job, an optimist sees the silver lining—in this case, perhaps a chance to pursue a more fulfilling career or hobby or take some much-needed time off. Optimists believe their actions result in positive outcomes, that they are responsible for their own happiness, and that they can expect more good things to happen in the future. Optimists don't lay the blame on themselves when bad things happen. They view adverse events as results of something outside themselves or, if a result of an action they took, they look for the valuable lessons in the experience. An unfortunate circumstance or event is viewed as a temporary setback—not a permanent way of life. Even if something dreadful happens today, a positive thinker believes good things will come again.

I always thought of myself as an optimist, and still do. However, when I lost the matriarchs of my family, for a while there it felt like the sun had set in my soul never to rise again. I thought God had decided to end all the amazing things in my life, and I didn't understand why. Thank goodness those devastating thoughts did not last forever. Thanks to all the lessons I had learned from those amazing women, I had the foundation to recoup my faith and hope for good things to come in the future. Optimism doesn't separate us from being realistic; it doesn't keep us from feeling sadness and grief or going through trying times. However, employing an optimistic mindset does give us strength to overcome challenges. The story we tell ourselves is everything.

The emerging field of positive psychology (which emphasizes

cultivating character strengths) highlights optimism's positive impact on mental health. Other research shows that optimism may be useful for our physical health, too. Studies suggest that optimists are sick less and live longer than pessimists. Apparently, a positive outlook on life strengthens the immune system (and the body's defenses against illness), cardiovascular system (optimists have fewer heart attacks), and the body's ability to handle stress. Optimists tend to share several positive characteristics that increase overall happiness and promote health, while reducing depression and chronic stress:

- They think about, reflect on, and emphasize the good things in life.
- They are grateful for all their blessings.
- They don't complain when something goes wrong.
- They feel that nothing can hold them back from achieving success and reaching their goals.

With the right attitude, these positive characteristics can be cultivated. Let's take a look at each more closely.

Emphasizing the Good Things in Life

This characteristic requires the ability or willingness to see the good in every situation. It can be as little as acknowledging that although it's raining on our picnic, the grass really needed a good watering. Or it can be something as life-changing as losing a job. Here's an example from my life:

Years ago, an exciting career in corporate America gave me the chance to work with some of the most influential firms in the world as well as some of the brightest people on the planet. Yet I wasn't feeling fulfilled. Although I had an incredible role in diversity and inclusion, an outstanding boss, an excellent team, and remarkable mentors, and I loved what I did every day, it still wasn't enough. Feeling unfulfilled and suffering from migraines several times a month (not to mention routinely missing Bible study), I prayed to God for direction.

Six months later, my mentors told me they were leaving the firm and one of our teams would be downsized. I felt confused, angry, and somewhat devastated. One of my mentors assured me he could find me a new opportunity within the firm. My other option was to use this as an opportunity to go on to do what I was destined to do, but I didn't know what that was. I ultimately wanted to teach, but I wasn't ready to earn the degree required.

My other mentor said, "Kim, go and do what you do, and that's help people. Go be a professional inspirational speaker or a corporate trainer or continue your work in diversity. Just do what lights your world on fire." Her words confused me. I thought I was already doing what lit my world on fire. (It is amazing how sometimes people see things in us that we don't see in ourselves. Just because we are successfully fulfilling a role does not mean we are walking in our ultimate purpose and life's assignment.)

The more I contemplated my mentor's words, the more I was convinced I had a choice to make. God had answered my prayer. Would I ignore it? Until this point, I thought I was doing every-thing I could for women and people of color to be noticed and have trajectories to C-suite positions. Instead of focusing on how upset I was that my mentors were leaving me and that I would be missing out on opportunities, I used it as a sign that it was time for me to do something different and recognized that this was a good thing. Today, through my advocacy and entrepreneurial efforts, I can do even more. Yes, I could have wallowed in my frustration, but instead, I used that energy to pivot! I launched my business, Reed Consulting Group and, thirteen years later, Reed Development Group.

Being Grateful for Our Blessings

Optimism is really all about adopting an attitude of gratitude. Practicing gratitude is the process of trying our best to see and be thankful for the positives in our lives, even in the midst of negative situations. It is about realizing that someone would eagerly trade places with us because our situation is better than theirs and, in fact, that many have it harder than we do.

As much as I detested having only forty-five days with my mom before God whispered in her ear to come with him, I am eternally grateful for each and every one of those days, moments, and memories. Some people die suddenly or lose their ability to communicate with their loved ones, so they don't have any time together at all. I had forty-five days. As I lay my head in my mother's lap while she took her last breaths, it would have been extremely hard for me to believe that anyone would trade places with me. Honestly, it is still difficult, but I do recognize the blessing of being able to do so and for that I am grateful.

Life is unpredictable. Don't wait for loss to find your voice to express your appreciation and gratitude. Take the opportunity now to more fully appreciate the blessings you have.

Not Complaining When Something Goes Wrong

Not complaining may be the hardest to accomplish on this list—especially if we are complaining about something we continue to tolerate. So, instead of merely not complaining—which is not easy at all, especially in these times of uncertainty—I suggest you give your mind alternative things to think about and give your voice something different to say. Here are some ideas:

- Recognize what people are doing right, and praise or thank them for the difference they are making.

- Listen to understand and learn. Don't look for reasons to shoot something or someone down. Instead, look for ways to build them up.

- Be responsible for your choices even if they didn't get you where you want to be. We will never become the best version of ourselves by living untested.

- Focus on your goals and achievements, and learn from your setbacks.

- Get active! Before you start whining, gossiping, or complaining, take a walk, go for a bike ride, or hit the gym. The idea is to get your body moving. Physical activity releases endorphins (the body's natural pain reliever). You are a lot less likely to complain with these tiny feel-good neurochemicals circulating in your body. If you don't know where to start, download a fitness app.

Being Serious about Achieving Goals (aka Personal Accountability)

Personal accountability is second nature to optimists. We take ownership of whatever we get involved in, and if there's something we want to achieve, we take action rather than just wish for it to happen. More than two decades ago, the *New York Times* bestseller *The Oz Principle: Getting Results Through Individual and Organizational Accountability* introduced readers to this powerful accountability philosophy. This is a good read if you are so inclined.

Redefine accountability for yourself. See it as a gift to yourself and a critical ingredient for achieving your goals. Staying true to yourself and your goals should not be drudgery. Write your goals down, say them to yourself, ask others to hold you accountable, and see yourself achieving them. That's the rocket fuel you need to catapult yourself into your C-suite.

Your *C-Suite* Life

C-suite (also known as *C-level*) describes high-ranking executive titles within an organization. The letter C stands for "chief." Officers who hold C-level positions are typically the organization's most influential members. Consequently, they set the company's strategy, make high-stakes decisions, and ensure the day-to-day operations align with the company's strategic goals. The number of positions and titles varies. Typically, larger companies have more executive positions to distribute the correspondingly larger workload. Three of the most common executives are the chief executive officer (CEO), chief operating officer (COO), and the chief marketing officer (CMO).

In your C-suite, you have five chief executives: the Chief Happiness Officer, the Chief Peace Officer, the Chief Wisdom Officer, the Chief Growth Officer, and the Chief Justice Officer. To bring them to life, imagine entering the spacious lobby of a magnificent building decorated to your taste. You feel right at home. A receptionist greets you and asks where you are going. You indicate you are headed to the executive level. She checks you in and hands you a special badge. You get on the elevator and soon arrive at your destination: the top level.

When you step off the elevator, you see that there are four large, beautifully adorned offices and a conference room. The names of the offices are Happiness, Peace, Wisdom, and Growth. There's one more office at the end of the hall: Justice. All the executives are meeting in the boardroom called Vision. Because you have a badge, you can freely walk around and peek inside the offices. These offices represent the highest-level qualities of their namesakes.

The Happiness Office

The Happiness Office is bright and sunny thanks to its huge windows with lots of natural sunlight. The executive in this office definitely gets their daily dose of vitamin D! We achieve the highest levels of happiness when we take the time to access and walk in our life's purpose. We get to define what makes us happy and place it in this space. If you dwell on what is *not* in your Happiness Office, it will become a cold, empty, dreary space. However, if you keep counting your blessings and recognize the gift you can be to others, this office will always be full of glowing, shining, beautiful light and joy.

There came a point in my life when I had to redefine happiness for myself. I grew up in Windsor, Connecticut, a suburb of Hartford, with the most extraordinary parents on this side of heaven. I also had amazing godparents and other loving, supportive family members. Like all families, we had our dysfunction but knew we could count on each other no matter what. I have beautiful memories of my childhood that positively shaped how I view the world and gave me a supremely optimistic outlook on life. Some would say that I walk through life wearing rose-colored glasses with a big bowl of sugar in my right hand.

My family always expected me to achieve great things. I followed the "happiness and fulfillment" blueprint that was laid out for me by everyone's expectations. I went to college, entered the workforce, and landed a job at one of the world's largest global professional services firms. I was a great performer, made a lot of money, cultivated incredible networking relationships/mentors, climbed to the top the right way, had an excellent career trajectory, met a cool guy, and lived in a chic apartment. *Voila!* I did what was expected of me with buckets of optimism, and all was well in the world.

In a sense, I had achieved half my goals. The other half of my goals—what I thought would make me truly happy—included a home with a light-brown picket fence that comfortably suited my family of three. However, after my cancer diagnosis and becoming single again, those goals seemed out of reach. That's when I had to redefine what I thought of as happiness. As an entrepreneur, I am driven, passionate, and love helping people achieve their goals. I rebuilt my C-suite Happiness Office with those elements instead of wallowing over the components that did not currently exist. I encourage you to fill your Happiness Office with the blessings that are present in your life now.

The Peace Office

The Peace Office is a soothing blue room with crystal vases, a comfy couch with luxurious pillows, and vibrant plants. The floor is covered in a plush gray rug with hints of silver thread. Lighting the room are gorgeous floor lamps that glow softly. This office is used for meditation, prayer, and relaxation.

We must cultivate the executive who occupies this office and visit this space on a daily basis. Many of the issues facing us today are rooted in the business of our lives. In 2020, our lives came to an unexpected, screeching halt on the heels of the COVID-19 pandemic. For many, not being able to have physical contact with family and friends, travel, work, shop, attend events, and generally be on the social scene led to anxiety, stress, depression, and loneliness. For others, it was a time to renew, reset, and focus on neglected areas of life. While it was likely a struggle for all, those who accessed this executive office fared better.

To experience peace, you have to build time into your schedule to rest, relax, and renew. For some, this is a walk on the beach; for others, it is uninterrupted time on a yoga mat; for others, it is prayer service at a place of worship. However you achieve the reset of your mind, body, and soul, it is essential to access this C-suite position. When you let go of the old ways of thinking, follow your bliss, and do what you love, you align with happiness and peace. These are all signals that you are connected to yourself in all ways. You are then allowing your real self to be the star in all its glory. Life is so precious and short. Spend it at peace not at war with yourself. Likewise, don't allow people to pull away your peace because another person took theirs.

The Wisdom Office

The Wisdom Office is a massive space that contains the most extensive library you have ever seen. Large desks are covered in a sea of books. From the Bible to the works of Socrates, Shakespeare, and other greats, this office is filled with opportunities to increase your knowledge and glean unimaginable wisdom. The wide perspective you have allows you to recognize and acknowledge differences in opportunities, people, behaviors, and more.

To fill this C-suite office, you observe, read, study, and learn. There are so many ways to glean information in the modern world—physical, digital, and audible. Learning from brilliant minds, virtually or in the classroom, is one way to gather wisdom. Another way is by consulting with good mentors, who you allow in this space often. A good mentor can save you time, energy, and money because they have already achieved what you wish to accomplish. Their success provides clues. Finally, the experiences you have throughout life contribute to the wisdom here, which, when you have access to this office, governs your life and sets a foundation from which you can help others.

The Growth Office

The Growth Office is a neutral, minimalist-style space that leaves plenty of room for embellishments. If there is too much in the Growth Office, nothing else can be added without creating clutter. When you have access to this C-suite office, you only fill it with simple, strategic, intentional pieces. When you do so, there is always room to shape it into whatever you need in the future. Growth can be transformational as well as painful. Growth is not just about growing our knowledge base, businesses, or careers; it also occurs when we look into our heart and mind and become intentional about how we want to live our lives.

The Vision Boardroom

The Vision Boardroom is a comfortable conference room with a large round table in the center of the space. Everyone on your executive committee has a chair at the table, and there are extra chairs for invited guests. This is a place where you chart your own destiny with all your C-suite executives on board. Sometimes outside leaders join the committee to provide guidance, and other times, you chart your course on your own. Here you have a solid plan for your life and goals to get you where you want to go. Your vision is the blueprint of what success means to you. Having a penciled in plan allows you to remain optimistic because it prevents you from the stress of floating through life like tumbleweed.

Justice Office

At first glance, the Justice Office is difficult to spot. You almost missed it as you explored the executive level. However, it takes your breath away when you enter. There's an array of magnificent oil paintings of those who have fought against injustice since the beginning of time. Among the paintings are famous Americans of color who fought against the pain and tyranny of racial oppression and injustice. You move around the room, and notice that the nameplates of each leader also includes the leader's quote on a powerful truth for the next generation. There are many portraits to view, but today, the following four stand out to you:

- The first portrait you see is a recent addition: U.S. Representative John Robert Lewis. He died on July 17, 2020, in Atlanta, Georgia, seven months after receiving a diagnosis of stage-4 pancreatic cancer. He was born on February 21, 1940, near Troy, Alabama. He was an American civil rights leader and politician. He was best known for his part in the landmark event in the history of the civil rights movement known as "Bloody Sunday." He was chairman of the Student Nonviolent Coordinating Committee (SNCC) and responsible for leading the march that was halted by police violence on the Edmund Pettus Bridge in Selma, Alabama, in 1965. Before that, he had the distinct honor of being the youngest person to speak at the 1963 March on Washington, which he helped organize in his role as chairman of the SNCC. He devoted his life to what he refers to as "good trouble" and encouraged the younger generations to pick up where he left off. His quote reads: "I believe in freedom of speech, but I also believe that we have an obligation to condemn speech that is racist, bigoted, anti-Semitic, or hateful."

• The next portrait you view is James Arthur Baldwin. Born on August 2, 1924, he was an American novelist, playwright, essayist, poet, and activist. His essays, as collected in the 1955 work *Notes of a Native Son*, explore intricacies of racial, sexual, and class distinctions in Western society, most notably regarding the mid-twentieth-century United States. One of his most significant achievements, which are too numerous to list, is that he is a direct creative descendant of the Harlem Renaissance movement. He died on December 1, 1987. Baldwin expressed his love for America with an honest rage and accuracy that is still relevant today. His quote reads: "Ignorance allied with power is the most ferocious enemy justice can have."

• Another Harlem Renaissance artist's rendering is positioned adjacent to Baldwin's painting. Langston Hughes's clarion call for the importance of pursuing art from a Black perspective was reflective of the Harlem Renaissance; additionally, it was the recurring theme of Hughes's work. Born in Joplin, Missouri, on February 1, 1901, he was an American poet, social activist, novelist, playwright, and columnist. Like Baldwin, Hughes's love for his country required that he hold the nation accountable for the atrocities people of color faced through his art. His nameplate is larger than the others because it has a short poem engraved on it fittingly titled "Justice":

That Justice is a blind goddess
Is a thing to which we black are wise:
Her bandage hides two festering sores

That once perhaps were eyes.

• The next painting is of Shirley Anita Chisholm, born on November 20, 1924. Her significance is credited by many as paving the way for Senator Kamala Harris to become the first Black woman and the first South Asian American woman to be named a vice presidential nominee on a major-party ticket in 2020. In 1968, Chisholm was the first Black woman to win a seat in Congress. Four years later, she ran for the Democratic presidential nomination against Senator George McGovern, pushing a platform focused on racial and gender equity. Another little known fact about her is that she is of Caribbean descent. Her parents were actually from Barbados, which is also a testament to all immigrants who are able to raise their children in America freely and proudly. She died on January 1, 2005. Her nameplate bears a short phrase that was both the title of her book and her campaign slogan: *Unbought and Unbossed.*

When you have access to this space, this part of your C-suite team is always guiding your actions. The Justice Room inspires you to seek justice for those who are oppressed in any myriad of ways in whatever small or large way you can. It also inspires you to support those who fight for justice. Knowing that additional portraits will be added to the walls as time passes gives you faith in and hope for the future. You say a silent prayer of thanks to those who dared to fight for us so that we can all access our own C-suite on our own terms.

A Story That Ended Without the Justice It Deserved

My grandfather Emmanuel Reed worked hard to provide for his family in Monroe, Louisiana, in the 1940s. He worked for a boating company where he drove a boat with cargo back and forth the river for very long hours. One day, two girls (the daughter of the owner of the boating company and her friend) needed to get to the other side of the river for a party, and they asked my grandfather to ferry them.

My grandfather said, "No, girls, I cannot take you in the boat— only cargo can go in the boat and it's too dangerous."

The girls didn't like his answer, so they told the girl's father that my grandfather was very disrespectful, mean, and flirty with them. After a long day's work, my grandfather returned home to greet his wife (my grandmother who was pregnant with my dad) and their children in the front yard. Several KKK members pulled up and got out of the car. They beat him to death in front of his family.

His young son Emmanuel never recovered from that racial trauma. One day, Emmanuel found one of the men who murdered his father—and I will leave the rest up to your imagination. Let's just say that when he came home, my grandmother packed up the children in the middle of the night, left everything, and headed to Ohio, where they made a home.

Exercise: Reflections on Your C-Suite Life

Set aside some time where you can be alone. Bring along a pen or pencil and your journal or notebook. Think about how your C-suite offices are currently decorated and what you are storing in those spaces, and respond to the following prompts:

- Office by office, make a list of all the positive things contained in them right now. These are all the good qualities and elements of your life.

- Which of your C-suite offices needs your attention? In other words, what do you need more of in your life?

- What's going on in your Vision Boardroom? List anything that might be standing between you and your goals. What will you do to overcome those obstacles? Remember, part of crushing your goals is having a clear, doable list. Remove any unrealistic expectations you have placed on yourself, but do make sure your goals challenge you to be and do your best.

- Write your goals on a separate piece of paper and look at them daily. Having your goals front and center remind you what you are working for and capable of doing.

Chapter 3

DISCOURAGEMENT ELIMINATOR 3:
Quiet the *Soul*

OUR SOULS CAN BE SADDENED by any type of loss, and the grief can feel overwhelming and overshadow the good things we still have access to. A loss can run the gamut from the death of a loved one or a loss of a way of life such as we've experienced with COVID-19, to a loss of health or a loss of social justice, and so on. Despite the circumstances going on around us and in our lives, our souls need a chance to access the quiet space inside us that is always at peace and knows that there is always hope for the future.

Here's a fair warning: You may need your tissues for this chapter. I still get emotional when I tell the story I am about to share with you. It took me a while to write it. Sharing our stories helps us process pain, and we must process pain before we can quiet our souls. The truth is that sickness is tough to handle, and the death of a loved one can be an ongoing source of emotional torture if our grief is not processed. This can be true for many types of losses.

Everything Can Change in an Instant

The craziest thing about life is that one day life can just be moving along amazingly well, and in an instant, everything can change.

On September 5, my thirty-ninth birthday, I was living an incredible life. I was thriving in my relationship with God, I had two extraordinary parents, and my mom was miraculously three years cancer-free from stage-IV endometrial cancer, the most common cancer of the female reproductive organs in the United States. God's power, faith, grace, glory, and optimism had prevailed.

I also had an abundance of love and joy, an incredible family, amazing friends (most of whom I called my sisters), a wonderful man I loved deeply and with whom I planned to build a future, a sensational career, and a growing business. I had it ALL! Life could not have been better.

I will always remember the day my dad called me with heart-stopping news. I heard the tremble in his voice. He said, "Kim, you need to come home, your mom is really ill, and she may die." I immediately responded with the same tremble in my voice that I would be there first thing in the morning. Though

I was scheduled to speak at an Urban League of Philadelphia event the next day, I canceled everything on my calendar for the remainder of the week and caught the train to Connecticut. As I packed, these questions flooded my mind:

How did we get here?

How didn't I know?

Is this why Mom and I haven't been talking on the phone as often and as long as we used to?

Why didn't I ask her if she was feeling okay?

How could I be so selfish?

Why didn't my dad tell me this sooner?

Die?

The only thing I knew for sure was that my mom simply could not die. With tears running down my cheeks, I collapsed on the floor and began to cry, "Please, please, Lord, please, Lord, do not let my mommy die. I need you to fix this. Whatever it is, you have my attention."

My mother and I used to talk multiple times a day. On the weekends, we could talk for hours, especially after church on Sundays. And, in between, we would trade fashion tips and advice. In the busyness of life, I had missed an important clue: our conversations had become shorter and more sporadic. I still carry a bit of guilt for not knowing that my best friend was smiling and being optimistic despite her illness.

When my dad met me at the train station the next day, he wasn't wearing his usual smile, and his arms weren't ready for a hug. He stood there looking sad, scared, and helpless. Holding back my own tears, I walked over, and he said quietly, "Hi, baby." He took my bags, and we got in the car for the ride home.

On the way, my dad quietly and slowly answered my questions

in a trembling voice. The "Queen of Joviality and Optimism" hadn't been to work in about two weeks, and her team and manager were worried about her. He explained that mom had an upcoming appointment to see the doctor, but basically they weren't sure what was wrong. She had lost a lot of weight and didn't have an appetite. Overall, she felt unwell. Part of me felt furious with my parents for not telling me what was happening at home, and this wasn't the first time they had done this.

A few months earlier my dad had had a mild heart attack, and my mom had rushed him to the hospital. He immediately went into surgery and had a stent inserted. (Thank God it wasn't more serious than a blockage.) On his way into surgery, he'd made my mom promise not to alarm me. So she waited until the next day to call to tell me what had happened. Though I could hear my dad in the background, sounding jovial and at ease, I cried hysterically. "Mom, how could you keep a secret like that from me? I am on my way now!" In response, I heard my father say, "No, Kimmie, I'm going home tomorrow, and your mother's got this! Just call me and check on me. I'm good." Meanwhile, we had no idea that my mom was sick.

I reflected quietly as these memories came flooding back. Though my dad had somberly prepared me for my mom's appearance, when I saw her, it took everything within me not to collapse. She was frail, about 100 pounds, and had a grayish hue. She was barely recognizable as the woman who would run downstairs as soon as the garage door opened to give me one of the biggest and best hugs on this side of heaven, accompanied by a booming, "Hey, honey!"

This time, Mom uttered the softest, "Hey, honey, how are you? You didn't need to come home." She gave me a feeble, short hug and then walked slowly back to the bed. My heart shattered into a million pieces. I had never felt so helpless.

The next day, to my surprise, Mom's appointment was at the Cancer Center. She was seeing an oncologist; her primary-care physician, Dr. Sherwood, my parents' doctor of more than thirty years, had referred her to Dr. Siegel, a top oncologist in Boston. Being a private person, my mom wanted to go into the exam room alone. I knew she was protecting us and operating in fear.

As I waited, I talked and prayed to God and tried to stay optimistic. Maybe she just had a nasty flu, I hoped. After about thirty minutes, she and Dr. Siegel asked my father and me to join them in his office. Dr. Siegal didn't have a bowl of sugar and said without a hint of optimism, "Your mom is very, very sick." When he told us that she needed to gain fifteen pounds in order to undergo any type of surgery by drinking Ensure and eating whatever she wanted, my mom asked in a soft voice, "What about the trans-fat, sodium, and calories?" And I was like, "Girl, nobody cares about calorie count! We have to put our boxing gloves on, get in the ring, level up our prayer, faith, and optimism, and fight whatever this is!"

Over the next several days, my mom had a series of appointments, including a biopsy and blood work. Determined that she would gain the pounds she needed, I practically bought the grocery store out of carbs, protein, and Ensure. I even bought a dozen blueberry doughnuts. After a few days of Ensure and tasty carbs, my mom was feeling better, the light had returned to her eyes, the grayish hue of her skin was giving way to her natural light brown complexion, her conversation was back, her laughter grew louder, and her hugs grew tighter. We'd won round one.

I made a quick trip home to get more clothes, take care of my mail, and plan for my sabbatical from my firm. My parents were going to need me, and not being by my mom's side was not an option. My mother began treatment for her cancer, and we all remained optimistic.

A few weeks later, though, my mom developed a severe condition as a result of the induction chemotherapy. All the optimism that had been anchoring my soul during this ordeal completely evaporated the moment I heard this news. I felt devastated and hopeless. The next morning, I arrived at the hospital around 7:00 to speak with Dr. Siegel as usual. He was simply amazing all during my mom's treatment, updating me regularly on her test results, next steps, and progress or decline.

When I visited early in the mornings, my mom would usually be sitting at the window, eating her breakfast, and waiting to greet me with her jovial, "Hey, honey!" Then she'd ask me for beauty supplies like her earrings, moisturizer, brush, ponytail holder, etc. Those days when she wasn't feeling her best, she would be in her bed rather than by the window, but the rest was as usual.

This day, when I got off the elevator, the nurse immediately greeted me. We had essentially become family with all the nurses who took amazing care of my mom and made it possible for my father and me to sleep at night. Her look of concern made my heart skip a beat. She said my mom had struggled a bit during the night and was exhausted. Her oxygen level had plunged into a danger zone, and she needed to wear an oxygen mask. She also wanted to prepare me for how she looked. Her glossy eyes would make her look sicker than she actually was, I was told.

With tears in my eyes, I pulled myself together. I knew Mom needed to see the sunshine in my face. She needed me to reflect back to her the faith, hope, and optimism she always had. I went into her room. She waved hello because it was hard for her to talk with the mask on. Then, hardheaded lady that she was, she removed the mask to say, "Hey, honey! What did the nurse tell you? She was so dramatic last night. I am fine. She came running in here while I was sleeping, Lord! It was not that serious."

We laughed. But I knew it was dire. All I could think and wonder was, *God, why are you allowing this to happen? Fix this, please. I am begging you to please heal my mommy.* My heart was breaking for my mom, and her heart was breaking for me.

Dr. Siegel knocked on the door, and this time, my mom asked me to go out in the hall to talk to him. Her spirit must have told her that this conversation was going to be different. Dr. Siegel was an amazing, caring doctor, but he *never* sugarcoated anything. We went into the hallway, and he said her oxygen levels appeared to be on the decline; he needed to know if she wanted to be placed on a ventilator should something happen. *A ventilator?* I called my dad, and he came right away. While we waited, Dr. Siegel and the nurses always told me it was hard to tell how my mom really felt because she always told them, "I am okay," or "This too shall pass." Her optimism levels during this season of her life were incomprehensible to everyone.

When Dr. Siegel explained the situation to my mom, her hand never moved from her Bible. Meanwhile, I was so angry with God. How could He let any of this happen?! I felt numb. Dr. Siegel said he wanted to move my mom to a "step-down" floor so she could get additional care. I packed up all of the pictures, balloons, all her stuff, and followed the nurses, the bed, and my mom to the step-down floor. Dr. Siegel told me it would be a tough day for Mom and our family. We would just have to get through the next twenty-four to thirty-six hours and get her oxygen levels up. Hopefully, things would get better, but they were not looking good.

My dad had arrived, and I told him all that I knew and tried not to break down in the hallway. We didn't talk in front of Mom because I wanted her to focus on breathing and getting better. My dad and I tried our best to hide our sadness and tears the best we could. That afternoon, a specialized doctor came by to help her breathe better but was unsuccessful. Doctors were in and out all day. My dad and I sat and talked with her, and at one moment, my mom looked at me and said, "Kimmie, it's bad, isn't it?" I said, "No, Mommy, we just have to get your breathing up, we will get there." I did everything to go to the depths of my soul to get that sheer optimism for my mom.

Next, they decided to do palliative care, which is the treatment of the discomfort, symptoms, and stress of any serious illness and help a patient deal with the side effects of medical care. Keep in mind, by this time, my mom was also fighting pneumonia. For seven days, she seemed to be getting better, but then things took a turn for the worse. The palliative medicine doctor came in to see my dad and me, but at this point, we were in a fog; we knew we were facing the inevitable. Just a little after midnight at 12:38, July 31, my mom passed away. I plunged into a state of enormous grief, and my soul cried out in agony. And that's where I would remain for a time.

Admit That You Are in Pain

The first step to healing from loss and trauma is admitting that you are in pain. Getting healed starts from understanding that you are in an unhealthy state. This step is similar to step one in 12-step programs: *admitting powerlessness over addiction.* Success in the program stems from the acceptance of that one key principle. You cannot change anything until you first admit and accept that it has a level of control over you. For the person battling addiction, it maybe some type of chemical or alcoholic dependency, but for the person who had just lost a loved one or is

suffering from another such trauma, that admittance and acceptance is that you cannot recover what you have lost and must take
the time necessary to grieve, to heal from the pain in your heart.

After my loss, I did not want to pray. I did not even want to
see a church. Like Job's wife in the Bible, I wanted to "Curse God
and die." That may sound extreme, but I was so angry with God
for taking my mom. I wanted to tell God that He had grossly
mismanaged His job. My healing came when I finally admitted to
myself that, yes, I was in pain and my grief needed time to heal, *I*
needed time to heal, and I needed to take steps to bring my soul
some peace so that I could once again tap into my faith and hope
and return to my optimistic outlook on life despite my tragic loss.

Take "Good Medicine"

I once listened to a preacher give a sermon on why bad things
happen to good people; at one point in the message, on the topic
of why good people die, the preacher joked, "Have you ever
wanted to give God a list of people you think He should go ahead
and take?" The congregation chuckled. This sermon made me
realize that laughter is a critical step to healing and quieting the
raging pain of the soul. Laughter is good medicine.

In *Emotional First Aid* by Guy Winch, Ph.D., the author com-
pares physical injuries to psychological ones. He says, "Loss and
trauma can shatter the pieces of our lives, ravage our relationships, and subvert our very identities." The experience of loss also
shatters your assumptions about the world, making you realize
that it's not as safe a place as you once thought. I can definitely
relate to this. When I lost my mom, it was if the whole world
stopped spinning. I was distraught, and it took me a while to
get myself together. To help my soul find some quiet, I turned

to humor. I cannot stress enough how important it is to laugh through the pain. Sometimes your tears and laughter will intermingle, and that is perfectly okay.

A few years ago, while doing research for a client, I clicked a hyperlink that took me to an article titled "Six Science-Based Reasons Why Laughter Is the Best Medicine" by David DiSalvo on *Forbes.com*. It's worth a read, but here's a summary to motivate you to make laughter a priority:

- Laughter releases feel-good chemicals called endorphins, which have an opioid-like effect without the downsides.
- Contagious laughers helps us bond socially.
- Hearing laughter exercises our brain.
- Couples who laugh together tend to have better relationships.

What's more, the University of Maryland Medical Center released a study in 2005 showing that laughter is linked to healthy function of blood vessels, which has a positive effect on cardiovascular health. Just think about all the hearts that could benefit from regular hearty laughter and other stress-reducing, joy-producing activities. So, while improving the health of your physical heart, laughter will dull the ache of your broken heart. Here are some ideas for adding more laughter to your life:

- Watch a comedy special.
- Spend time around little kids; nothing will heal your heart like the infectious laughter of little ones.
- Click on those funny duck, puppy, goat, hippo ... you name it ... videos.

- Recall humorous incidents from your life and share them with someone.

- Got to a comedy club or watch one of your favorite comedians.

- Read a funny book or article.

Whatever you do, make it your business to laugh daily and often. It is a wonderful way to lighten your heart and ease feelings of grief.

Make Positive Declarations

No matter what caused your pain, making positive declarations daily can help you navigate your feelings and regain a positive perspective. You can use your favorite scriptures, positive quotes, and/or write your own affirmations. The key is to say it until you feel it, and then once you feel it, keep saying it until you can live it. Some of my favorite declarations are taken from scripture. I'll share them with you here:

Because I place my hope in the Lord
my strength is renewed.

—Isaiah 40:31

God causes all things to work together for good
to those who love God, to those who are
called according to His purpose.

—Romans 8:28

So with you: Now is your time of grief,
but I will see you again and you will rejoice,
and no one will take away your joy.

—John 16:22

The LORD is close to the brokenhearted and
saves those who are crushed in spirit.

—Psalm 34:18

Blessed are those who mourn, for they will be comforted.

—Matthew 5:4

This is the day the LORD has made.
We will rejoice and be glad in it.

—Psalm 118:24

As much as I miss my mom, I am glad that she is no longer suffering. I would not have wanted her to hold on for me while struggling to breathe and in pain. That is not who my mom was. I will always remember her as a spunky, vibrant, classy lady who brought sunshine to every room she entered, and my memories of her will always bring me joy. As John 16:22 says, "No one will take away your joy."

Display Your Beautiful Memories

When your soul is raging with grief, you can quiet it with beautiful memories. If you've lost a loved one, it may be difficult to look at mementos and photographs right away, but I encourage you to do so as soon as you are able. Create a place where you can display your memories in physical form—a rock from the beach you picked up when you were together, a photograph of you and your loved one in happy times, etc. Maybe you can decorate a wall or shelf with items that make your soul feel connected to your loved one.

With regard to other losses, you can still remember the times you enjoyed that person or thing. What might spark beautiful memories of what you no longer have? Get as creative as you need to be to remind yourself of the good times. Being reminded of happy times can help you feel more optimistic about your ability to make happy memories in other ways in the future.

Be an Active Participant in Quieting Your Soul

At the end of your life, would you regret having lived your life in a state of perpetual despair? Probably. So do what you need to do to push past your despair. Whether you pray, meditate, or exercise, you need to be an active participant in your soul's quieting. Any or all of these activities can help your soul find the peace it craves so that you can finally get out of the sea of negativity you may be drowning in.

If you feel comfortable praying but have not done so in a while, take up the daily habit again. If you've never prayed before but would like to, you may find comfort there. The same is true for meditation. Likewise, some people find that exercise helps them clear away the residue of grief. Do what works for you—and your soul.

Talk about Your Pain

No matter what type of loss you may be grieving, it helps to talk about your loss and your pain with trusted friends and family. Sometimes it takes a trained professional to help you recover and reignite the joy that's waiting on the other side. If you feel you cannot work through your grief alone, I urge you to find someone to talk to. There's no reason to go it alone.

Grieving Over the Loss of a Parent?

The loss of a parent is a painful, difficult experience we will all likely encounter in our lifetimes. I lost my mother, and I've known women who have lost theirs, and we've shared how hard and heart-wrenching this loss has been. The mother-child bond is unique. My mother gave birth to me. She fed and nurtured me throughout my childhood. She was always there for me when I needed advice or had a problem. She was not only my greatest advocate and best friend but part of my soul. I even looked like her. She was the most remarkable woman ever, and I wanted to be just like her. When she passed, I felt like I'd lost part of my soul.

I have been blessed to have very close relationships with both of my parents, and my heart breaks for those who have a strained or nonexistent relationship with their parents. If a parent should pass before amends can be made, the unresolved issues can make the grieving process that much tougher. Many people are surprised at how much the loss of a parent affects them. Their friends and family perhaps won't realize just how big a blow it can be, especially if the parent was old or ill for a long time, and it was expected.

Grief over a parent's death can be one of the hardest things we face in life, but nearly all of us have to face it at some time. Everyone's grief is different, and we all have our own ways of coping. We may feel some or all of the emotions of sadness sometimes, or we might just feel numb and blank. If your grief is long lasting and you feel you cannot go on without your mom or dad, I encourage you to speak with a grief counselor soon.

Exercise: Explore Your Beliefs

Go someplace where you can be alone. Take along your journal or notebook and respond to the following prompts:

• What does "quieting the soul" mean to you?

• What is a soul? What are the qualities of your own soul? How does your soul feel during the most painful times in your life?

• Do you pray? If so, how important is prayer in your life? What was the last thing you prayed about?

• Do you meditate? If so, how important is meditation in your life? When was the last time you meditated? How did you feel afterward?

• Does your spirituality have a direct connection to your outlook on life? Write about the link between spirituality and how you view the world.

• What is your favorite scripture, quote, or affirmation? How do you apply it to your life?

Chapter 4

• •

DISCOURAGEMENT ELIMINATOR 4:
Have *Gratitude*

"Gratitude is the rocket fuel to our resilience."

—Kimberly S. Reed

WHEN I THINK ABOUT the most challenging days of my life and how I persevered, one word comes to mind: *Gratitude*. Gratitude fuels both our resiliency and our faith. As I write these words, the amazing actor Chadwick Boseman just lost his battle with cancer at the young age of forty-three. The media has been highlighting his amazing career, but I am more impressed with his ability to continue pursuing his life's purpose even in the face of his greatest challenge. I imagine that he lived each day in gratitude, which gave him the resiliency to move forward with his life's work.

Like Chadwick Boseman, I choose to be grateful for each day I get to live. I also choose to be grateful for the limited time I had with my mom in her final days. I have found that gratitude is the most powerful way to access our optimism. The ability to be thankful for all things is a surefire way to achieve individual greatness. Gratitude also enables us to connect to something larger than ourselves, whether to others, nature, or a higher power. What's more, gratitude sets us up for additional blessings.

Gratitude So Great It Garnered Heaven's Attention

One of my favorite stories about being thankful is found in Luke 17:11–19 (AMP). It reads:

11 *While Jesus was on the way to Jerusalem, He was passing [along the border] between Samaria and Galilee.* **12** *As He entered a village, He was met by ten lepers who stood at a distance;* **13** *and they raised their voices and called out, "Jesus, Master, have mercy on us!"* **14** *When He saw them, He said to them, "Go and show yourselves to the priests." And as they went, they were [miraculously] healed and made clean.* **15** *One of them, when he saw that he was healed, turned back, glorifying and praising and honoring God with a loud voice;* **16** *and he lay face downward at Jesus' feet, thanking Him [over and over]. He was a Samaritan.* **17** *Then Jesus asked, "Were not ten [of you] cleansed? Where are the [other] nine?* **18** *Was there no one found to return and to give thanks and praise to God, except this foreigner?"* **19** *Jesus said to him, "Get up and go [on your way]. Your faith [your personal trust in Me and your confidence in God's power] has restored you to health."*

Now, I am not sure what made the other nine lepers go on with their lives. However, this one leper refused to receive his healing without going back and giving thanks to the Healer who made his physical miracle possible. As a result, his praise and worship were recognized and acknowledged by the Messiah. I do not know about you, but I want my gratitude to be so great that it garners attention from Heaven!

Notice that Jesus acknowledged the leper who fell at His feet and thanked Him. At no point in the story does Jesus ignore him and wait for the other nine to come back before He speaks words of blessing over the man with gratitude. Let that be a lesson for us as we attempt to do nice things for others. Often, we become so focused on the people who did not thank us for our acts of kindness that we miss the joy we created for the people who benefited and showed thanksgiving. The same way the one leper could not make the others come back and thank Jesus, you cannot force anyone to be thankful. The only thing you can do is make sure you are a person of gratitude.

The Goodness in the Now

Some people miss great blessings in their lives because they are always looking for the next good thing without acknowledging the goodness in the *now*. Being grateful for our blessings in life is the key that opens the door to an optimistic life of success and prosperity, while a lack of appreciation often keeps us feeling down.

The most critical component of showing gratitude is to make the decision to be thankful. When we appreciate what is in front of us right now, life gives us more to enjoy. Have you ever been around someone who constantly complains they are short on time? Their complaints rob them of the opportunity to enjoy the time they do have. Remember being a kid and begging for just "five more minutes" and becoming instantly unhappy if it wasn't granted? That unhappiness robbed us of the ability to appreciate the time we did have.

You Just Keep Living, Baby

My parents taught me many lessons (for which I am grateful!), and expressing gratitude was high on the list. I went through forty years of my life without any earth-shattering adversity, feeling blessed and grateful for those blessings, while those around me lost loved ones and suffered other emotional traumas. I might have been inclined to ask, *Does my life really deserve this level of blessing? Was my level of sin so low that God did not allow me a season of strife? What did I do that was so freaking amazing that I get to live this amazing life?* I remained grateful for my blessings.

On the flip side, following those first forty years, I survived challenges so intense that I would not wish them on my worst enemy. Am I less grateful for my blessings? No. After experiencing a significantly overwhelming season, I learned what the older generations meant by the phrase, "You just keep living, baby." If you live long enough, life *will* dump adversity on you that drops you to your knees. And Lord knows, I found that to be true! We just get back up and keep on living.

While I could have focused on the negatives when my illustrious job in corporate America came to an end, I chose to greet the future with optimism and gratitude for the lessons learned. I pivoted and started Reed Consulting Group (now called Reed Development Group) in 2007. I had a nice severance from my previous employer, which enabled me to start my business. I made $4,231.13 in my first year. How did I live off $4,231.13?

The severance package certainly came in handy, and my gratitude for that cushion was immense! I saved the W2 from that year to remind me where God brought me from and to remind me how blessed I am. When we accumulate wealth over time or through an extensive process, it keeps us humble and grateful for the abundance.

Expressing gratitude is a lot like avoiding complaining. When we stop complaining about all the things we don't have, that we think we deserve and instead focus on what we *do* have, life pivots. Think about farmers. In the past, when we lived from farm to table, whether or not it rained was much more significant to our daily lives. If the fields went too long without rain, an entire village could starve. Today, however, rain is often seen as a nuisance, when the reality is that life could not exist on earth without water. Therefore, we must learn to enjoy the rain and be grateful for it while waiting patiently for the storm to pass. We do this knowing that something is being watered in our "life garden" even though the showers may be unwanted or inconvenient. There is wisdom in recognizing the significance of the storm and being grateful for it.

Gratitude has a way of continually redirecting our focus. When we are thankful, our mind shifts from what we think we should have more of to the abundance that is already present. When that occurs, we can begin to eliminate excess. We accumulate possessions when we are unable to see that true beauty is not in more but is actually in less. Purging the unnecessary from your life, whether it's getting rid of junk in your garage, ending toxic relationships, recycling what's outlived its purpose, or making room in your heart for new love is empowering.

Once you do this, you are genuinely ready to make each day count. You will be able to wake up and live your day with purpose.

Again, I'm reminded of Chadwick Boseman. Even after being diagnosed with colon cancer, he still made *seven* successful movies. His blockbuster hit *Black Panther* reported earnings of $1.3 billion at the worldwide box office and won ninety awards. This is significant because it is proof that, no matter what you are facing in life, unimaginable success is possible when you link up with a winning team. Can you imagine enduring surgeries, treatments, and intense pain and still getting up and going out to inspire others and provide for your family? What if Boseman, instead, had focused on his loss of good health and chose to turn his back on his life's purpose? We would not have been graced by his talent or his example of living life to its fullest. I hope his example encourages you to think about how to get the most out of your life each day.

Expressing Gratitude Through Words and Actions

If we are going to be grateful, it helps to apply words and actions to our gratitude. There are many ways to show our gratitude and keep discouragement at bay. In this section, I'll share some ways you can express gratitude for each day you are aboveground. Chadwick Boseman's passing at such a young age, along with the manner others who have lost their lives seemingly too soon, is a somber reminder that none of us knows just how many days we have here on the earth. The key is to live each day filled with gratitude and thanksgiving. Let's look at some ways to do that.

Show Up

Give *100 percent* of yourself to whatever you do every single day. I want you to take a moment now to open your internet browser and look up the song "99 1/2" by Gospel singer, song-writer, and pastor Hezekiah Walker. First read the lyrics and then take a listen. The song opens with "Lord, I'm running tryin' to make a hundred because ninety-nine and a half won't do." If you know anything about Gospel music, you know that choir lyrics often repeat throughout the song. One listen and it's doubtful you will forget it. Even if this isn't your kind of music, the song holds an important message: It is critical to do whatever we are called to do with all our heart, mind, and soul. This is how we show God our gratitude for our life and our gifts. There is no need to "half-step" as we used to say back in the day—show up and go hard every single day.

Master Your Craft

Chadwick Boseman played some of the most memorable and historical Black characters. Not only did he bring those characters to life, but because representation matters, he also inspired millions of black and brown children. However, he would have never been cast in those roles if he wasn't able to embody every character he played. Let his example inspire you to do the same.

Whatever your purpose is, whatever you are passionate about, dedicate your entire being to it. Once you learn it, master it. Mastering your craft is more than becoming an expert in your field or industry, although that will certainly be one of your main priorities. Mastering your craft also means knowing how to use your product or services to bring solutions to the people you strive to help or retain as clients. There is no better way to show gratitude for a gift, skill, or ability than by mastering it to make the world a better place.

Volunteer

A great way to express gratitude for what you have is to share your time and talent with organizations or individuals who may not be able to afford your services. On their website, the Mayo Clinic lists six benefits of volunteering, among them are a decreased risk of depression (especially for individuals sixty-five and older), a sense of purpose, the opportunity to learn new skills, mental and physical exercise, and reduced stress. What's more, volunteering with at-risk populations can help you better understand how blessed you truly are.

I once heard someone say that people who live in third-world countries say that Americans are so wealthy that even their cars have homes. This confused me until I realized they meant garages. Before then, I had not considered that a garage could be perceived that way by someone with less fortunate circumstance, and I never forgot that lesson. We do have so much to be grateful for; sharing ourselves and our blessings with others is a great way to remain humble and express our gratitude.

Give

When was the last time you made a contribution to a local nonprofit, a charity, your place of worship, or your college alumni association? People in our communities everywhere are attempting to make a difference, but they need our financial support. I am not suggesting you dig a well, but I am suggesting that you consider foregoing a simple luxury (one night of going out to dinner, for instance) to be able to give a donation that could impact someone else's life in a significant way.

Researchers suggest that giving to others may improve physical health and longevity because it helps decrease stress. Because no one is immune to stress, I highly recommend giving as one way to alleviate it! Additionally, in a 2006 study by Rachel Piferi of Johns Hopkins University and Kathleen Lawler of the University of Tennessee, the researchers said that "people who provided social support to others had lower blood pressure than participants who didn't, suggesting a direct physiological benefit to those who give of themselves." If better health isn't reason enough, giving also helps you leave a legacy for the next generation. You never know how the funds you donate will change someone else's life forever.

Many of us have heard the common scriptures about money: "The love of money is the root of all evil" (1 Timothy 6:10) and "Will a man rob God? Yet, you have robbed me in tithes and offerings" (Malachi 3:8). A while back, I stumbled upon this one: "A feast is made for laughter, And wine makes merry, But money answers everything." (Ecclesiastes10:19 NKJV)

I was blown away by this one because it is saying that in addition to faith and work, we also need access to finances because money can *answer* all things (not that it is for all things). That means some people need us to show our gratitude for what we have been given by allowing our finances to answer a need in their lives.

Become a Mentor

Have you benefited from the help of a coach, mentor, teacher, or networking connection? If so, find a way to help the next generation to make their path a little easier. We have all heard the expression, "It is not what you know, but who you know." Who is benefiting from your connections? Who have you helped up a rung on their career ladder lately? If you cannot answer those questions, I suggest you get started.

You never know how many lives you can impact for the better by becoming a mentor to someone. You will also be establishing an overflowing fountain of gratitude in your own life—especially if you are a minority. Men and women of color have a far more difficult time climbing corporate ladders than anyone else. One of the tragedies of our time is that glass ceilings still exist based on skin color. You could be the person who destroys that glass ceiling looming over your mentee's head. I encourage you to get busy making a difference in as many lives (or at the very least one) in your particular industry as possible.

Exercise: Gratitude Journey

Find a quiet spot where you can be alone with your journal or notebook. Respond to the following prompts:

- How can you start practicing gratitude on a daily basis? Write about all the ways you can think of and then put a plan in motion.

- Gratitude today creates vision for tomorrow. Make a list of things you believe are standing between you and feeling grateful for what you have. What do you plan to do about it?

- Accept your current situation and where you currently are in life. You may not be where you want to be, but practice being grateful for where you are and acknowledge that you're still trying. Write about all the things in your life right now that you are grateful for.

Bonus activity: Start a "gratitude bag." Get a shopping bag from your favorite store or buy a special bag. For the next forty-five days, write one thing that you are grateful for on a piece of paper. Below that, write about how you plan to maintain it or continue to nurture it in your life. You can even take a photo of whatever that thing is, print it out, and put it in your bag with your notes. At the end of the forty-five days, take a look at all you have to be grateful for!

Chapter 5

DISCOURAGEMENT ELIMINATOR 5:
Have Faith at the Speed of *Light*

IN HEBREWS 11, it says "Faith is confidence in what we hope for and assurance about what we do not see." Faith at the speed of light is allowing faith to envelop you without question or debate. We never know what storms await us or when our faith might be tested. In the blink of an eye, it could be our season. We need to have unyielding faith in order to walk through our season with optimism. Remember, having faith is not about being *certain* of an outcome, but knowing that whatever the outcome, it is ultimately for the best, even if we can't recognize it as such. It's knowing that we have the strength to get through whatever test life puts before us. That is true optimism. Nothing discourages pessimism as much as having faith in the ultimate good.

My Mother's Example of Deep Faith

I tossed in bed for hours. I looked at the clock, and it felt like time was literally standing still. I had to get up in two hours anyway. Everyone would start calling to ask if I needed help getting ready. I couldn't even tell them how much I was struggling or how I was broken to the core, because "Kim Reed" was always supposed to be on. Ironically, the same disease that had caused the funeral I would be attending in a few short hours was also now raging within my body.

We all make decisions to protect those closest to us by keeping the truth from them for as long as we can. My mom had done it. My grandmother had no idea that my mom's cancer had returned. She didn't want me to tell her, and I would not violate her trust. I lay there wondering if I would truly ever recover from this loss. I thought it had been tough going, sitting at her side and praying for her to get better. That heaviness was nothing compared to the emptiness of her being gone... forever.

I still remember that morning so vividly all these years later, yet everything that followed is a series of blurs. I remember hugging my father. I remember the emptiness in my grandmother's eyes. I remember the flowers and even their strong scents. I remember the cards—so many of them. So many hugs and various perfumes, and yet I can't recall one single fragrance because they all blended together, as if walking by a department store perfume counter. It was the absolute worst day of my entire existence. Even those days when I suffered from cancer myself didn't compare. Those days are over, and I am healed, but my mom is forever gone.

The last forty-five days of my mother's life taught me more about myself and about faith and trust than I had learned in my forty years on earth. Following her cancer diagnosis, she experienced ups and downs in her health but not in her outlook. Her strong faith remained steadfast. I watched her walk through an experience most people half her age would barely be able to endure: seven days of induction chemotherapy, twenty-four hours a day. Even in her darkest hour, she still depended on a higher power and had faith so deep that even in the midst of her pain, treatments, and discomfort, she never complained—not once. I also never saw her shed a tear. My mother was a real-life Wonder Woman. Of course she had days when she did not feel well, but the optimism in her voice and spirit never wavered.

During that time, my mother transferred her strength to me, and I hope to pass that strength along to everyone who reads these words. She showed me what "unexplainable trust" looks like. As it says in Proverbs 3:5–6: "Trust in the LORD with all your heart, and do not lean on your own understanding. In all your ways acknowledge him, and He will make straight your paths." I could never have conceived before that time that such trust was possible. I learned so much from her example by listening and watching how to have strong and deep faith when it was time for me to fight my own battle a few months later.

The Roll Call of Faith

As women, it can be tough for us to access our inner strength. We have come as far as we have thanks to all the women (of all races, nationalities, ethnicities, and religions) who came before us and stood up for us so that our lives would be better than theirs had been. Many risked everything for what they believed.

In Hebrews 11, you will find the "Roll Call of Faith." The roll call includes all the biblical characters who lived by faith, among them Noah, Abraham, Moses. Their unwavering faith is inspiring, and their teachings are critical to my faith. Here, though, I want to share with you a roll call of strong women who accessed their strength and lived in faith. Read more about them when you need inspiration and encouragement to keep on going, trusting that you are making an important difference.

- **Joan of Arc**—Joan of Arc is regarded by many as one of the bravest women in history. As the English army was poised to invade France, Joan of Arc rallied the French troops to an unlikely victory in the siege of Orléans. She, too, was a woman of faith. She truly believed that she was on a mission from God to defeat the British and actually fought. As a result of her conviction, she changed history forever. My favorite Joan of Arc quote is: "I am not afraid...I was born to do this."

- **Rosa Parks**—A roll call of faith would not be complete without Rosa Parks; she is another example of the rare and extreme bravery of women who transformed history. Parks refused to give up her seat on a segregated bus, resulting in the Montgomery Bus Boycott, a watershed moment in the American Civil Rights movement, and ultimately led to the end of segregation in the United States. Parks has become an iconic symbol of standing up for what is right, and her actions have inspired countless other women to do the same throughout the world. Parks was a little spark (she was only five feet, three inches tall) who ignited a fire of change. When interviewed years later, she said, "People always say that I didn't give up my seat because I was tired, but that isn't true. I was not tired physically, or no more tired than I usually was at the end of a working day. I was not old, although some people have an image of me as being old then. I was forty-two. No, the only tired I was, was tired of giving in."

• **Mother Teresa**—This next lady is so cemented in her cause for helping the poor that the name "Mother Teresa" is actually used to describe an individual who advocates for the poor. Mother Teresa Bojaxhiu was a leader of a group of nuns in India. She was courageous because she not only devoted her life to making the lives of the sick and impoverished in the world better, she wrote and spoke to others and helped give a human face to the issue of poverty. Mother Teresa changed history by inspiring countless people to help improve the lives of the poor and sick worldwide. She was one of the first people I learned about who devoted her life to advocating for those who were both distressed and destitute. She recognized her most extraordinary ability was to be an instrument of God's love on the earth. You can see that in her own words: "I'm a little pencil in the hand of a writing God, who is sending a love letter to the world."

• **Amelia Earhart**—A woman who found success in a male-dominated field in history was the pioneering aviator, Amelia Earhart. She was the first woman to fly solo across the Atlantic Ocean. This was an extremely courageous act that affected history because her resilience and bravery inspired generations of women to pursue previously unobtainable dreams. As she flew across the skies, she changed the limits of what women believed they could accomplish. Earhart tried to fly around the world, but her plane disappeared, and nobody knows what happened to her, but her abilities and accomplishments still inspire women, even today.

- **Mary Jackson, Katherine Johnson, Dorothy Vaughan, and Others**—Equally as fascinating as Earhart was a group of women who happened to be NASA's best-kept secret. For decades, female NASA employees dubbed "computers" helped the United States excel in the space race. Still, their critical contributions remained largely unacknowledged, not only outside NASA but also within it until the hit movie *Hidden Figures.* The blockbuster hit introduces three of these women's stories: Mary Jackson, Katherine Johnson, and Dorothy Vaughan. While their stories are compelling, the work of their colleagues who still remain in history's shadows was also of great importance. You can learn more about all of them in the 2016 book *Hidden Human Computers: The Black Women of NASA* by Sue Bradford Edwards and Dr. Duchess Harris (whose own grandmother was one of the "computers").

All of these women's accounts span decades, but having strength, tenacity, faith, and courage is nothing new. As a matter of fact, the woman who embodies all of these characteristics ultimately is an unnamed woman in the Bible. Yet, her story is so significant that it appears in three out of the four gospels—Mark, Luke, and Matthew. She is simply referred to as "the woman with the issues of blood." When I was in at the lowest point in my valley, I began studying her.

She lived during biblical times, so her gender alone relegated her to the position of second-class citizen. She would have been considered "ceremonially unclean" based on Old Testament Levitical Law because she was bleeding. Additionally, not only was she suffering with a terrible condition, but also, no matter what doctor she went to, her problem only got worse. She lived with this condition for twelve long years without relief. At some point, she learned that Jesus was coming to town, and while she would have been able to have a conversation with Him legally and logistically, she reasoned that all she needed to do was touch his garment, and she would be healed.

Can you imagine having that type of faith? Can you imagine believing in a higher power's ability to help you reverse a condition you have been plagued with for over a decade? I do not know what you may be battling or struggling with, but I believe a powerful supply of faith like this woman's can be developed when you practice the optimism-cultivating tools in this book. Try to see yourself in her shoes. Try to put whatever difficulties you are having behind you and believe in a better outcome. Make a decision to have faith that healing your heart, mind, body, and soul is possible. A belief in a higher power is all that's required; it doesn't have to be Jesus if that's not your religion. But for now, let's explore this woman's story more deeply:

The Gospel of Mark provides the most detailed account:

A woman in the crowd had suffered for twelve years with constant bleeding. She had suffered a great deal from many doctors, and over the years she had spent everything she had to pay them, but she had gotten no better. In fact, she had gotten worse. She had heard about Jesus, so she came up behind him through the crowd and touched his robe. For she thought to herself, "If I can just touch his robe, I will be healed." Immediately the bleeding stopped, and she could feel in her body that she had been healed of her terrible condition.

Jesus realized at once that healing power had gone out from him, so he turned around in the crowd and asked, "Who touched my robe?"

His disciples said to him, "Look at this crowd pressing around you. How can you ask, 'Who touched me?'"

But he kept on looking around to see who had done it. Then the frightened woman, trembling at the realization of what had happened to her, came and fell to her knees in front of him and told him what she had done. And he said to her, "Daughter, your faith has made you well. Go in peace. Your suffering is over."

—Mark 5:25–34 (NIV)

This woman had spent every last penny she had to get better, but a cure still alluded her. Fast-forward a couple millennia, and it's still the same story. Many people are drowning in medical bills trying to be cured of or treated for their ailments. In fact, as of April 2020, it is reported that the number of uninsured Americans is currently more than 27 million and is expected to rise. Many people must pay out of pocket for medical treatment and/or the medication they need. It takes strength and faith to get through challenges like that. If you relate, take heart in knowing you are not alone and realize that we are stronger together. One of the ways you can contribute is to share "optimism and strength" stories like this one.

Let's now look at Luke's account of the story (Luke 8:43–48 NIV) where he adds a notable distinction:

> **43** *And a woman was there who had been subject to bleeding for twelve years, but no one could heal her.* **44** *She came up behind him and touched the edge of his cloak, and immediately her bleeding stopped.* **45** *"Who touched me?" Jesus asked. When they all denied it, Peter said, "Master, the people are crowding and pressing against you."* **46** *But Jesus said, "Someone touched me; I know that power has gone out from me."* **47** *Then the woman, seeing that she could not go unnoticed, came trembling and fell at his feet. In the presence of all the people, she told why she had touched him and how she had been instantly healed.* **48** *Then he said to her, "Daughter, your faith has healed you. Go in peace."*

Keep in mind that Luke was a doctor by trade, and medical professionals do a pretty good job of getting straight to the point! He did not give us nearly as many details as Mark did, but he did point out in verse 47 that, in the presence of all the people, she explained *why* she had touched Jesus. This is significant because even though we live in a world where people highlight all their wins on social media, most hide their struggles and difficulties. This woman who was considered "unclean" and struggling financially boldly told an entire crowd of people of her suffering before she had touched Jesus and how she had become instantly healed.

Imagine if you were in that crowd. Even if you were not facing a struggle such as hers, her testimony would surely be an experience you would never forget. It would be a story you could put in your memory bank to recall and apply anytime you needed it!

The other remarkable part of Luke's account is that "she did it afraid." He says she was trembling as she spoke. This speaks to the fact that not every circumstance in our lives will be met with bold, confident action. It is often a tiny, timid step of faith that makes a bigger difference than a daring leap of faith. Never be ashamed of crawling before you walk or walking before you run. The important thing is that you get up every day and keep going, regardless of the pace.

Let's now turn to Matthew's brief account of her story in Matthew 9:2022 (NIV):

> **20** *Just then a woman who had been subject to bleeding for twelve years came up behind him and touched the edge of his cloak.* **21** *She said to herself, "If I only touch his cloak, I will be healed."* **22** *Jesus turned and saw her. "Take heart, daughter," he said, "your faith has healed you." And the woman was healed at that moment.*

These three different accounts of the story is like hearing the same news story on CNN, Fox News, and your local news channel! The most notable portion of Matthew's brief account is that Jesus encouraged her *before* He healed her. This is a beautiful reminder that God's delay in answering our prayers is not a denial. Most of the trials we face have an expiration date; we just have to keep moving forward, trusting in the higher power that fuels our faith.

I love that Jesus uses the words "take heart" in Matthew's account. On this journey from defeat to life's C-suite, we all need to take heart. When we are struggling, we must remind ourselves often to take heart—specifically to:

- Feel encouraged.
- Allow our blessing to bolster our confidence, courage, and happiness.
- Be confident.
- Be brave.
- Feel happy or hopeful.
- Feel more positive about something.
- Have more courage or confidence.
- Cheer up.

Never Forget: Your Voice Matters!

Keep in mind that biblical stories as well as much of our history was written by men. We live in a world where our stories are often told by people who do not look or think like us. It is imperative that women and minorities, in particular, be determined and resolute about sharing their life experiences with others in their own words. You never know whose life will be changed because they have heard you tell your story. You may have lived through something that might make someone else want to give up until they hear that you have lived through a similar experience and made it out on the other side!

Strong Faith Is Vital for Challenging Seasons

I learned from my mother that unyielding faith can help us have peace in this life, even as we are transitioning to the next. As she lay fighting for her life, she held on to her faith.

Two days before she died, my mom prayed for her pneumonia to be taken away. The night before she died, as I was leaving the hospital, I asked her, "How are you feeling, honey?" She replied, "You know, Kimmy, I tell you I don't...well...I just wish...well...I want this pneumonia taken away from me." And I said, "Okay, I'm going to be in agreement with you." Then I kissed her goodnight, and she hugged me tight and she told me how much she loved me. What still stings for me about this particular time is that her wish came true and not mine. She did not have pneumonia for her last day on earth. She was not completely coherent, but she was not in pain. She slipped into a peaceful sleep. Even to this day, I am still in awe of how she was healed, and we were able to have breakfast together that morning before she started her transition.

My mother's passing was incredibly tough for me. After some time had elapsed, a conversation with my aunt helped me get myself together and put things in perspective. She pointed out that had my mother continued to live in her condition, she would not have been able to do all the things she had loved to do: see my grandmother in Boston once a week, go on vacations with me, visit me in Philadelphia, chat on the phone while she was at work, and more. I mean, the woman literally never sat still! She was outgoing, enjoyed her job, loved her church, and even took kickboxing classes! She did it all. After that conversation, I understood that my mother's preordained task on earth had been carried out. I believe that each of us is preordained to carry out a specific purpose on earth, and in some instances, the end of people's lives hold more valuable lessons than the ones they articulated while vibrant and healthy.

When you tap into the level of faith my mom displayed at the end of her life, you know that you can feel optimistic through any challenge. You *can* experience joy no matter your circumstances. Remind yourself why it is important to build your faith by saying the following: "I need to develop strong faith *before* the trials come so that I can lean on my faith during difficult times. I never know when difficulties will arise; I just know that they will. I need to practice faith at the speed of light so I can live my life with optimism." I highly recommend writing that statement on a sticky note and reading it every day. Then, take steps to build your faith by "taking heart."

Before we get to the exercises for this chapter and close out our discussion on faith, I want to share a note with you from my beloved aunt that I hope will inspire you on your journey. I believe it will be a blessing to you, just as it has been a blessing to me.

A Note of Love and Optimism from Remarkable Auntie Rose

> *"A man's heart deviseth his way; but*
> *the Lord directeth his steps."*
>
> —Proverbs 16:9

Growing up, I had many ideas as to how my life would one day be played out. During those young years, I had seen and heard of numerous life stories that were quite unappealing to me. My mind became busy thinking about the thing I would or would not do to effect the happy results I imagined for myself. So like a playwright, I began the task of creating the stage and script for my story.

Time passed. Life was fairly good. I graduated high school, college, and became gainfully employed. I had fallen in love back in high school and that happiness continued to the point that I became engaged. We got married, honeymooned, and returned home on "cloud nine" where I just knew we would always reside.

While we continued to interact with family and friends—we were the principle characters in each other's lives. God remained at the center, and we were so thankful that he had blessed us to be together. Gradually other characters began appearing on stage. They were beautiful, cuddly, sweet, and numerous. We were in awe, and with God's help, we dove into the parental arena with passionate love and seriousness. My dream was seemingly on point.

However, overtime, our "cloud" became cluttered with an array of life's issues. So cluttered, in fact, that it began a noticeable descent and finally hit earth with a loud thump. In my dream world, this was not supposed to happen. Tiredness, frustration, and sacrificing took up residence as we became inundated with diaper changing, late-night feedings, potty training, doctor and dental appointments, homework, school projects, peer pressure, and rebelliousness. As diligently, as we strove to live Godly lives and to pave Godly paths to be followed—some of us, at one time or another, chose to go off script. In addition, our family experienced illnesses, deaths, broken relationships, joblessness, financial woes, and the like.

Oftentimes, I would reminisce about those dreams I had many years earlier, and for a brief moment, I would suffer a degree of disappointment. However, as I grew as a Christian, I came to understand that my dream was *not* reality for it was out of my real-life experiences that my spiritual fruit tree grew and God produced in me a better person for His honor and Glory.

With the stroke of a pen, it is so easy to write a beautifully unmarred script. But as we produce our stage and script—we must never forget that God is sovereign and that he alone occupies that Director's chair. As our Director, we can rest assured that, in spite of failed dreams, he can cause all things to work together for good.

Challenges will continue, but recognizing that absolute supremacy of God, counting our blessings, giving thanks, and living with hope remain the priority of the day. With this in mind, we can all approach life with an optimistic and winning attitude.

Love,
Auntie Rose

Author's note: Auntie Rose's eldest daughter, my cousin Donna Tarber, passed away in June 2020. Despite this terrible loss, her strength is commendable and her faith is to be admired.

Exercise 1: Identify a Great Example

In a quiet place with your notebook or journal in hand, sit quietly for a few moments and bring to mind one person in your life who has deep faith. Respond to the following prompts:

- What are some of the characteristics this person has that has seen them through difficult times?

- What are some of the habits they practice to maintain their strong faith?

- In what ways can you put those same habits into practice in your life to strengthen your faith so that you can call upon it when you need it?

Exercise 2: Reframe a Past Disappointment

After you've completed exercise 1 or at another time, sit quietly for a few moments and think about a time when you felt deeply disappointed that your prayer wasn't answered or a desire you had did not come to pass. Respond to the following prompts:

- List all the details you can remember about the event or situation, being as objective as you can.

- In what way(s) did not getting your prayer answered the way you wanted it to turn out for the better?

- Reframe your disappointment by letting go of what you wanted to happen and seeing the good that came out of it. Write a paragraph or two about it from an optimistic viewpoint.

Chapter 6

• •

DISCOURAGEMENT ELIMINATOR 6:
Unlock Your *Y.E.S.*

DO YOU KNOW THE STORY OF ALADDIN? Many movies have been based on this centuries-old folk tale, most recently the 1992 and 2019 Disney versions. In a nutshell, Aladdin is a poor kid who finds a magic lamp, rubs it, and a genie appears and grants him three wishes. As is usually the case with genies and wishes, Aladdin doesn't make great choices.

Aladdin is a lot like us. He knew what he wanted, but he had no idea how best to achieve his goals. Before we are too hard on poor Aladdin, we must admit that we have all been in his curly-toed shoes. Many of us have made bad decisions because we lacked understanding, mindfulness, and/or self-awareness. However, these are crucial components needed to make the best decisions. They enable us to unlock our Y.E.S. factor: *You Empower Self.*

Awareness and Acceptance

Unlocking your Y.E.S. factor—empowering yourself— requires mindfulness. While you can find this term defined and described in a number of sources, one of the most straightforward definitions I came across was on the *Psychology Today* website. It describes mindfulness as "a state of active, open attention to the present. This state is described as observing one's thoughts and feelings without judging them as good or bad."

Two essential components are needed to achieve mindfulness: awareness and acceptance. Awareness is the knowledge and ability to focus on your inner processes and experiences, such as the present moment's experience. Acceptance is the ability to observe and accept—rather than judge or avoid—those streams of thought. As I write this book, we are in the midst of the COVID-19 pandemic where life is so unpredictable and different from what we were used to. If there was ever a season to become more mindful, this is it. Mindfulness can certainly help us navigate this uncertain journey and keep us from spiraling into negativity.

Whether you make a structured mindfulness practice part of your routine, such as a daily mindfulness meditation, or just make an effort to become more aware of what's going on inside you and note it without judgment so that your decisions are made from a place of balance, you are taking important strides toward your personal empowerment and setting yourself up to help others unlock their Y.E.S., too. But *you* come first!

Why Self-Care Is Essential

If you are always running around helping everyone else, I am giving you permission to do something for yourself. I want you to pause here and go get a cup of tea, a smoothie, or whatever beverage soothes you. Go ahead, I will wait. It is critical to become serious about self-care—especially for women. We often take care of everyone but ourselves, and we must do better. One of the issues women face as a result of stress and lack of balance is that it increases their heart disease risk. According to the American Heart Association's initiative Go Red for Women:

- An estimated 44 million women in the United States are affected by cardiovascular diseases.

- 90 percent of women have one or more risk factors for heart disease or stroke.

- Women have a higher lifetime risk of stroke than men.

- 80 percent of heart disease and stroke events may be prevented by lifestyle changes and education.

- Fewer women than men survive their first heart attack.

Minorities face even greater risks:

- Hispanic women are likely to develop heart disease ten years earlier than Caucasian women.

- Hispanic women are least likely to have a usual source of medical care, and only one in eight say that their doctor has ever discussed their risk for heart disease.

- Cardiovascular diseases are the leading cause of death in African-American women, killing over 48,000 annually.

- Of African-American women ages twenty and older, 48.3 percent have cardiovascular disease. Yet, only 14 percent believe that cardiovascular disease is their greatest health problem.

Being aware and informed can assist all of us in making small everyday changes that will help us live more enriching lives. This is important because I have been affected by the devastating challenges that can develop from living an unbalanced life. Fortunately, I was able to successfully overcome the difficulties, but I know many other women who were not as fortunate. After meeting women who had attempted suicide because their lives had become overwhelming to them and knowing several family members who suffered severe stressors that led to heart disease and strokes (many under age fifty), I concluded that I needed to do my part in educating women on the threats of living an out-of-balance life with regard to their physical, mental, emotional, and financial well-being. Regularly practicing self-care can help you bring these life factors back into balance.

Exercise: Rate Your 30 Days

Take a minute now (no need to wait till the end of the chapter!) and reflect on the last thirty days of your life. On a scale of 1 to 10, with 1 being "horrible," 5 being "decent or mediocre," and 10 being "one of the best months of your life," give your last thirty days an honest rating. Now, let's unpack that rating a little. In your notebook or journal, respond to each of the following prompts:

- What did you rate it and why?

- What were your wins? What made you happy or grateful?

- What were your woes or worries? Were there any setbacks?

How do you turn "ones" into "fives" and "fives" into "tens"? You begin by making yourself a priority. In the same way a flight attendant instructs passengers to put on their own oxygen mask before helping others, you need to take care of yourself before you can take care of others. If you are low in the self-care department and you are running out of oxygen, chances are you are also running low on optimism. I want you to have high-scoring months all the time, so read on!

Empowerment Starts with You

The first thing you need to know about the Y.E.S. factor is that before you can empower others, you have to be satisfied with yourself. If you want to spread encouragement, optimism, and love, you first need to feel those things about yourself. If that sounds selfish, consider the Buddhism's four divine states of being: loving-kindness (*metta*), compassion (*karuna*), empathetic joy (*mudita*), and equanimity (*upekkha*).

There is a meditation practice designed to cultivate each of these emotions. *Metta* focuses on the self, and practitioners start with a message of self-empowerment:

May I be happy. May I be healthy and strong. May I be free from anger, hatred, animosity, resentment, and ill will. May I experience real peace, real happiness, real love.

Karuna, or compassion, results directly from *metta*, and focuses on other people, with the idea that what you manifest for yourself, you're then able to display for others:

May you be happy. May you be healthy and strong. May you be free from anger, hatred, animosity, resentment, and ill will. May you experience real peace, real happiness, real love.

Empathetic joy is being happy because other people are happy and equanimity is being in a state of calmness, thereby completing a circle that begins with self-empowerment.

The Difference between Self-Respect and Selfishness

When you devote time and energy to empowering yourself, people may criticize you or hurt your feelings by trying to convince you that your actions are selfish. Those people are wrong. Self-respect and selfishness aren't only different; they are opposites. When you are selfish, you are looking for something that's not good either for you or for anyone else. If you're doing something because it makes you—and only you—happy, you'll ultimately be left with nothing but guilt, and you'll have given away your power to positively impact others. Selfishness means you can't set an example, be a leader, or inspire.

Self-respect is the opposite. It means putting your own empowerment first on your list of priorities and doing things that make you happier and more fulfilled and, by extension, increase those feeling in the people around you. Most important, the more you build your self-respect and self-empowerment, the more you set an example for others. Positively impacting others' optimism and fulfillment is the polar opposite of selfishness—and that all begins with you.

Respecting Yourself, Your Life, and Others

When you respect yourself, you begin to understand your value and your strength. It also helps you understand how you can best share your gifts and talents with the world. You know what you bring to the team, you have confidence in your value, and you contribute to the overall success of the group.

Once you achieve self-respect, you are ready to apply respect to every aspect of your life. When you respect your life, you begin to focus on your goals in a specific way. You move past the trivial things. There are so many people who end up losing because they got stuck on foolish and inconsequential matters. But when you have genuine respect for your life, you realize that you matter and what you do has the power to impact others.

Significant action in life requires a team, and to acquire the best team, you must find the value in other people. One way to always experience the best in others is by understanding reciprocity. Reciprocity requires us to give trust to gain trust. Additionally, it requires us to give love to receive love. Finally, reciprocity requires striving for agreement so that we can attain agreement.

The Power of Words

I cannot stress enough the importance of being careful with the words you speak. Becoming empowered begins with how you process your feelings and emotions; those emotions becomes thoughts; and those thoughts become words. Your words confirm your feelings as truth.

Another response with regard to the words you speak is to start edifying. When you edify, you are speaking the truth from a place of love. You are not using your mouth to speak death, pain, and hurt. Say what you need to say in order to help, inspire, and build others up. You're not going to have a successful relationships in business or otherwise if you're cursing everybody out! Yes, you've got to tell the truth, but you've got to do it with love. Once you practice speaking the truth this way, you will see the quality of your relationships increase and your optimism will spill over into those around you.

To inspire you, here are nine of my favorite quotes on the power of the words:

"Be careful what you say. You can say
something hurtful in ten seconds, but ten years later,
the wounds are still there."

—*Joel Osteen*

"Be mindful when it comes to your words.
A string of some that don't mean much to you may
stick with someone else for a lifetime."

—*Rachel Wolchin*

"Before you speak let your words pass
through these three gates: Is it true?
Is it necessary? Is it kind?"

—*Rumi*

"For me, words are a form of action, capable of
influencing change. Their articulation represents
a complete, lived experience."

—*Ingrid Bengis*

"If you talk to a man in a language he understands,
that goes to his head. If you talk to him in his
language, that goes to his heart."

–*Nelson Mandela*

"Handle them carefully, for words have
more power than atom bombs."

—*Pearl Strachan Hurd*

"Words are containers for power, you choose
what kind of power they carry."

—*Joyce Meyer*

"The six most important words: I admit I made a mistake.
The five most important words: You did a good job.

The four most important words: What is your opinion?
The three most important words: If you please?
The two most important words: Thank you.
The one least important word: I."

—*Anonymous*

"When a thoughtless or unkind word is spoken,
best tune out. Reacting in anger or annoyance will
not advance one's ability to persuade."

—*Ruth Bader Ginsburg*

Exercise: Choose Different Words

Think about your most recent complaint. Let's say you went to a restaurant, and when your dish came, the vegetables were overcooked, your pasta was more than a little al dente, and the chef must've dropped the salt shaker in the sauce. When you leave, you might be inclined to say, "That restaurant was terrible!"

Seems reasonable, but it is also very negative. You could say, "I've had better!" Both statements may be true, but one has a much more positive ring to it. You've basically said what you wanted to say without putting negative energy through your body—you even used a positive word to do it!

In your notebook or journal, list various verbal negative responses to adverse situations that you have said or you have heard other people say. Then, for each statement, choose different words to say what you want to say without using negative words.

The more you practice positive responses, the more positive you will become overall.

Turning Tragedy into an Empowering Movement

Here's a message I shared with my social media followers: "Our positive life situations and seasons aren't the cause of our happiness; they are the result of our happiness. Our love, joy, inner voice, peace, and happiness come from knowing we are enough." It's important to internalize this lesson as you embark on a mission to cultivate optimism in your own life and spread it to others. It can be detrimental to your well-being if you shift your focus to other people before you've done the required work on yourself; you can only give from what's available, and if your well isn't full, it's more likely to run dry. You will simply not be able to help others or help empower them if you don't feel empowered. The only way to get the kind of authenticity that allows you to inspire others is through self-empowerment. Love you, first.

Of course, this self-empowerment message can be easier said than done, and it doesn't just happen overnight. It is important to continue empowering yourself by empowering others, especially after you have faced extreme hardship or loss. For example, in 2008, Jennifer Hudson's mother, brother, and nephew were murdered by her sister's estranged husband. Hudson was able to turn a tragedy into a powerful vehicle for giving back to her community. Along with her sister, Julia, the singer started a charity in memory of her nephew, Julian King. The Julian D. King Gift Foundation's mission is to "provide stability, support, and positive experiences for children of all backgrounds to help enable them to grow to be productive, confident, and happy adults." The organization collects and distributes school supplies, toys, and clothes for children who are in need.

Hudson has also been involved with organizations dedicated to combating violence against women and girls, which is critical considering the number of women who suffer at the hands of violent partners. Domestic violence stats from the National Coalition Against Domestic Violence (NCADV) reveal that:

- Every nine seconds in the United States, a woman is assaulted or beaten.

- On average, nearly twenty people per minute are physically abused by an intimate partner in the United States. In one year, this equates to more than 10 million women and men.

- One in three women and one in four men have been victims of (some form of) physical violence by an intimate partner within his or her lifetime.

- One in five women and one in seven men have been victims of severe physical violence by an intimate partner in their lifetime.

- On a typical day, more than 20,000 phone calls are placed to domestic violence hotlines nationwide.

- The presence of a gun in a domestic violence situation increases the risk of homicide by 500 percent.

- Women between the ages of eighteen and twenty-four are most commonly abused by an intimate partner.

- Nineteen percent of domestic violence involves a weapon.

- Domestic victimization is correlated with a higher rate of depression and suicidal behavior.

- Only 34 percent of people who are injured by intimate partners receive medical care for their injuries.

- Seventy-two percent of all murder-suicides involve an intimate partner; 94 percent of the victims of these murder-suicides are female.

- One in fifteen children are exposed to intimate partner violence each year, and 90 percent of these children are eyewitnesses to this violence.

- Victims of intimate partner violence lose a total of 8.0 million days of paid work each year.

- Between 21 and 60 percent of victims of intimate partner violence lose their jobs due to reasons stemming from the abuse.

- Women abused by their intimate partners are more vulnerable to contracting HIV or other sexually transmitted infections due to forced intercourse.

- Negative physical, mental, sexual, and reproductive health effects have been linked to intimate partner violence, including adolescent pregnancy, unintended pregnancy in general, miscarriage, stillbirth, intrauterine hemorrhage, nutritional deficiency, abdominal pain, and other gastrointestinal problems, neurological disorders, chronic pain, disability, anxiety, and post-traumatic stress disorder (PTSD), as well as noncommunicable diseases such as hypertension, cancer, and cardiovascular diseases.

- Victims of domestic violence are at higher risk for developing addictions to alcohol, tobacco, or drugs.

- A potential relationship exists between intimate partner violence and depression and suicidal behavior.

Sure, that's a lot to be pessimistic about. However, optimism is knowing that when we act together and empower each other, we can change those disheartening statistics. It all begins with awareness: You can get more information and find additional resources on *acadv.org*.

Another example of someone flipping tragedy into an opportunity to serve others is Joaquin Phoenix. While Phoenix is widely recognized for his portrayal of musician Johnny Cash in the 2005 movie *Walk the Line*, many do not know that he lost his nineteen-year-old brother River to a drug overdose. After facing negative media following the incident and taking time away from acting because of it, Phoenix suffered from his own substance abuse problems. After successfully completing rehab, he has maintained his successful acting career. He is on the board of directors for the Lunchbox Fund, a nonprofit organization that provides daily meals to students in Soweto, a town in South Africa. He had served as a dedicated social activist for PETA (he's vegan, too), Amnesty International, The Art of Elysium, HEART, and the Peace Alliance. You can learn more about all of these organizations with an internet search.

Yet another example is actor Tyler Perry, who was officially added to *Forbes'* list of billionaires in 2020. Perry's childhood struggles included physical and sexual abuse. Inspired by Oprah Winfrey in the early nineties, he wrote and produced a play about child abuse survivors, losing all his money in the process. For a time, he lived on the street. The show eventually went on to make him millions—and, as this rags-to-riches story goes, Perry is now a billionaire. What is hugely significant about this is that Perry is one of the *most* charitable celebrities today, often helping his Atlanta community as well as people whose stories draw his attention. He is a wonderful example of empowering himself and then empowering others.

During the COVID-19 pandemic, Perry gifted 1,000 Kroger supermarket gift cards to those living in Atlanta with the help of the Atlanta Police Department, whose officers went door to door to hand out the cards. In August 2020, he donated a van to an Atlanta women's organization that provides hygiene products to people experiencing homelessness. In April 2020, he paid for the groceries of elderly shoppers at forty-four Kroger stores in Atlanta and twenty-nine Winn-Dixie stores in his native New Orleans. During the writing of this book, he also announced that he would be paying not only for the funeral of Rayshard Brooks, the Atlanta man who was killed by a police officer on June 12, 2020, but also for the college educations of Brooks's four children. In this way, Tyler Perry actively uses his blessings to be a blessing to others.

Now, I know that these three examples are of celebrities, and we can't all fall into the spotlight this way, but our efforts toward empowering others and supporting the causes we believe in is just as important and significant. Every effort counts.

Voices of Self-Empowerment

Empowerment doesn't work like a light switch; it's not just on or off. It's something you have to continuously work at, and it starts with your voice and the voices you choose to surround yourself with. In my personal and professional life, I make a concerted effort to surround myself with voices who inspire optimism and provide examples I want to emulate. I find time to read inspirational books almost every day—even when my schedule is busy, overwhelming, or totally crazy. I also watch inspirational artists and speakers on YouTube. I listen to people like life coach Tony Robbins and researcher and speaker Brené Brown. I let their voices get into my spirit and soul, and I meditate on their words and ideas.

This is what I mean when I say that others can play a role in self-empowerment. Sometimes, hearing others explain why we are worthy help us internalize and personalize the message. In a TEDx Talk that I've returned to several times, Brené Brown explains that what you believe about yourself is what you put out into the world, and it makes up what you receive. In "The Power of Vulnerability," she says:

> *I wrote a book, I published a theory, but something was not okay—and what it was is that, if I roughly took the people I interviewed and divided them into people who really have a sense of worthiness—that's what this comes down to, a sense of worthiness—they have a strong sense of love and belonging—and folks who struggle for it, and folks who are always wondering if they're good enough. There was only one variable that separated the people who have a strong sense of love and belonging and the people who really struggle for it. And that was, the people who have a strong sense of love and belonging believe they're worthy of love and belonging. That's it. They believe they're worthy.*

And you are worthy! We all are, but sometimes, we need to be reminded. Some self-help folks often tell you to speak words of affirmation to yourself in the mirror. However, mirrors don't show who you are within, which is the you that needs empowering. Talking to yourself won't change your non-empowering behaviors. Yes, surrounding yourself with empowering voices, including your own will help, but what's really going to change your behavior is *taking action*. This is vital and critical to being and remaining self-empowered. Very often, the difference between getting it done and not getting it done is whether or not you have the right tools.

The more empowered you feel, the more you believe you are

capable of accomplishing goals...and the more you expect from yourself. If you've built up your self-respect and self-worth, your belief in yourself won't be misplaced: It's not just that you *think* you can do more; you will be *able* to do more.

Your attitude defines your environment. If you're feeling incapable or insignificant, that will become your reality. Negativity closes your mind to possibility, and your opportunities plummet. Once you reach the peak place in your self-empowerment journey, you've entered the realm where everything suddenly becomes possible. Your possibilities for success increase exponentially in the world of empowerment you've created.

There's a quote attributed to Mahatma Gandhi that has been printed and reprinted so many times it has become a cliché: "Be the change you wish to see in the world." The truth is that while this is not precisely a misquote, it has been condensed and paraphrased. It is easy to interpret the quote as meaning that if there's something you see as a problem in the world, you should take it upon yourself to change it. But what he really said isn't just about the actions you take; it is a lot more literal than that. Gandhi was suggesting that we could change the world around us by elementally changing ourselves. Here's what he said:

> *We but mirror the world. All the tendencies present in the outer world are to be found in the world of our body. If we could change ourselves, the tendencies in the world would also change. As a man changes his own nature, so does the attitude of the world change towards him. This is the divine mystery supreme. A wonderful thing it is and the source of our happiness. We need not wait to see what others do.*

Inspiration is necessary, and it helps to surround yourself

with empowering voices, but you know what you need, and you know what feels right—mind, body, and soul. Trusting yourself to pursue only what fuels your sense of happiness and fulfillment will set you up to aggressively pursue your goals and eliminate self-doubt, which will drag you down and keep you from being able to be a blessing and an example for others. Learn to forgive yourself for those doubting thoughts; we all have them, and when they pop up, the best thing you can do is to identify their source and stop them in their tracks. You can learn to turn those moments around: When you begin to feel self-doubt, stop and ask, "How can I turn this into empowerment? How can I become the change?" And then take action.

An Intentional Environment

My life changed for the better when I became intentional about my environment, including my living space. Becoming intentional about one's environment can mean a lot of things, but here's one example of what this might look like for someone.

After the May 2020 protests following George Floyd's death, my associate wanted to become intentional about self-empowerment and his environment. For this guy, it meant recertifying for his concealed weapons permit. It also meant purchasing a new firearm and making weekly trips to the gun range for target practice. He said he was changing everything in his life, starting with his bedroom. Curious, I asked him to tell me more. He explained that he had watched a video in which Colion Noir—American gun-rights activist, lawyer, and host of the widely popular web series *Noir*—took his viewers step-by-step through his bedroom to show how it gave him a superior advantage over intruders. (Talk about intentional!) Noir's nightstand houses a MacBook, a multidevice-charging station, a gun case that is unlocked by thumbprint application (gun fully loaded, with one already in the chamber), a super-bright flashlight, and more. As extreme as this sounds, my friend slowly set up his bedroom according to Noir's setup, and now he say he sleeps more peacefully because his environment gives him the best possible vantage point in the event he has to contend with an intruder.

While I'm not suggesting a setup like this is necessary to feel empowered, I am suggesting that we can all adjust our environments to empower ourselves in a way that makes sense to us. My friend was able to sleep more peacefully with the adjustments he made, and likewise, when we are intentional about our environment, our dwelling is more peaceful and joyful, and we naturally feel more empowered.

Does your living space cultivate calm and peaceful thoughts? Does it make you feel like when you leave it, you can go out an accomplish amazing feats? If not, start taking small steps to re-create your environment. It isn't necessary to get into debt to remodel your space. Make a plan and execute it a little at a time. Pick a soothing color for your walls, and pay attention to proper lighting. According to the California Lighting Technology Center, "An adequate amount of light improves mood and energy levels, while poor lighting contributes to depression and other deficiencies in the body. The amount and type of lighting directly affect concentration, appetite, mood, and many other aspects of daily life." In general, we need different types of lighting. I suggest using light bulbs of differing wattages and installing blinds to let light in and blackout curtains to keep light out.

Keep in mind that none of the adjustments you make to your living space and your greater environment matter if you don't have a healthy routine. The COVID-19 pandemic forced a lot of people to retreat into their living spaces, rest, and reset their lives. What's working in your daily routine? What isn't? Be sure to review your routine seasonally, as well. Depending on your line of work or general lifestyle, some periods of your life may look very different from others. The same way most businesses do quarterly or annual reviews, I suggest you do this for your life. What better place to reflect than in the intentional space you have set up for yourself through careful planning and thoughtful execution. This keeps you connected to your Y.E.S. factor.

Who Is in Your Living Space?

Do you have a partner or roommate who is robbing your atmosphere of joy and peace? If so, unlocking your Y.E.S. factor will be a superhuman feat. A poorly chosen partner will (intentionally or inadvertently) try to pull you and everyone else down to their level of discontent and unhappiness. The old adage "misery loves company" is unfortunately accurate. I have also learned that success will always breed envy around the wrong people. How do you keep that negativity from seeping into your environment and derailing your journey to empowerment? You don't get angry or expect different from people who exude negativity.

As the venerable Michelle Obama told us, "When they go low, we go high." You act on your empowerment, exude optimism, excise toxicity, and "be the change." And often, the change requires a parting of ways. Too many of us stay in bad friendships, partnerships, and relationships for way too long, unable to pull the trigger on the gift of goodbye. However sometimes the first step to intentionally adjusting your environment is actually changing *who* is in it.

Exercise: Your Y.E.S. Factor

Spend some time reflecting on the following prompts. Once you have had a chance to think them through, use your journal or notebook to record your thoughts on each, being as specific as possible.

- What is your biggest goal for your life?
- What is missing from your life? What do you need more of to thrive?
- What makes you feel enlightened and uplifted?
- What do you think the world needs more of right now?
- What do you think the world needs less of right now?
- What does self-empowerment mean to you?
- What does empowering others mean to you?
- What makes you happy?
- How do you feel about your life right now?
- What changes are you planning to make in your life?
- Does any area of your life feel unempowered or incomplete? If so, how?
- How will you change your environment so that you can feel more at peace and joyful?
- Here is the big one: Think about the past couple of years. Did you make yourself any promises you didn't keep that you think would make you feel more fulfilled?

Bonus activity: Seeing your dreams and goals each day reminds you what you're working for. Think of an innovative way to showcase your goals. Will you make a vision board? Write affirmations on colorful sticky notes? Start a photo log? Get creative.

Chapter 7

DISCOURAGEMENT ELIMINATOR 7:
Give What You *Require*

HEALTHY, RECIPROCAL relationships help us feel supported and encouraged in life, setting us up for a more positive view of the future. Everyone has an unspoken agenda when it comes to relationships—whether it's with friends or love interests. We all require love, loyalty, trust, care, support, and encouragement from others. But the other half of the equation—the part that makes it possible for us to get those things—is on us. We have to be willing to make deposits into our relationships if we want to get those qualities from them. Let's take a look in this chapter at the balance between giving and receiving in your relationships.

Relational Equity

One of the best ways to always get the most out of your relationships is to simply give what you require. Relational equity is one of the most valuable elements you could ever achieve. Think of your relationships and your networks, both personal and professional, as your investment portfolio. When you invest your money, the smart thing to do is choose stocks that you believe will grow your wealth. At the very least, you don't want to end up with less money than you started with. A diverse financial portfolio includes a mix of investments: Some are risky—those could bring you significant benefits *if* they pay off. Others are more dependable; they may not make you filthy rich, but you can rest assured you'll get back what you put in.

I will not claim to be a romance expert. I'm a single woman. But I have had several loving relationships, and using what I've learned about investing in friendships and business relationships, I've built a thriving business and a sterling professional reputation. I've always prided myself on my network, and I recognize its importance. In fact, one of my favorite sayings is, "Your network is your net worth." But as I get older and observe relationships that work for all parties involved, I have learned that relationships are really a series of investments, deposits, and withdrawals.

I know a married couple who was really struggling in their marriage and were sadly heading toward divorce court. Six months later, when I saw the wife, she seemed happier than ever. I thought that maybe she had a new love interest, but I was incorrect. The married couples' ministry at her church started reading a book that changed her life. It was called *His Needs, Her Needs* by Dr. Willard F. Harley.

I asked her the concept that made this book so transformational for her marriage, and she started explaining Dr. Harley's "love bank" theory to me. To be sure I explained it to you thoroughly, I cross-referenced my interpretation with Dr. Harley's website, where you can read the full explanation: *www.marriagebuilders. com/the-love-bank.htm*. Dr. Harley summarizes it like this:

> *Inside all of us is a Love Bank with accounts in the names of everyone we know. When these people are associated with our good feelings, "love units" are deposited into their accounts, and when they are associated with our bad feelings, love units are withdrawn. We are emotionally attracted to people with positive balances and repulsed by those with negative balances. This is how our emotions encourage us to be with people who seem to treat us well and avoid those who seem to hurt us.*

Dr. Harley explains that when there are more withdrawals than deposits in marital relationships, couples no longer want to live their lives together and eventually grow apart. I believe this is true not only for romantic relationships but also for all relationships.

We have to see all relationships as investments that can become over withdrawn if we continue to make debits without deposits. This concept should be applied this way: to be willing to give if we want something in return. We cannot expect love or other positive characteristics if we are not willing to give them. We simply have to be willing to put in the work to build healthy relationships because they are vital to our lives. The deposits create and facilitate meaningful connections and continue our ability to grow together. "By the time you're a social worker for 10 years, what you realize is that connection is why we're here," says Brené Brown. "It's what gives purpose and meaning to our lives. This is what it's all about. It doesn't matter whether you talk to people who work in social justice, mental health, and abuse and neglect. What we know is that connection, the ability to feel connected—neurobiologically, that's how we're wired. It's why we're here."

Evaluate Your Connections

Now it is time to evaluate your connections. Are your relationships all returning your investment? Are you depositing your love, care, attention, and energy in the right places? As you begin to take stock, you need to internalize an important point: Everybody is not your project, and you can't make deposits with no return forever. At some point, you need to recognize that it's time to stop. You have to take an inventory of what keeps you optimistic and examine your relationships in that mix. Your relationships are invaluable to your life, and they're what will either hold you back or propel you forward. Your relationships are your currency, and you need to make choices about how to keep that currency safe, help it grow, and put it to work for you.

Deposit Before You Withdraw

This may seem like a no-brainer, but there's nothing you can take from an empty account. Maybe you've heard the expression, "You can't draw blood from a stone." If you want something out of a relationship, you have to be willing to put equally as much into it, or more.

When you're depositing in the right places, you begin to feel all of what you're putting in. You feel the support, encouragement, and love. We don't give to get—that's not what this means—but in a relationship, you *have* to meet someone halfway. That doesn't always mean you're getting and giving equally. Sometimes, it means things are 50/50, sometimes it's 80/20, and that's all OK. The pendulum swings and people count on one another for different things at different times. Whether it's with a friend, a family member, or a colleague, you'll know your relationship has healthy deposits when that person is happy, and you are equally satisfied as well. They're happy about being there for you, clapping for you when you win, and you celebrate their success as if it is your own.

Nurture Your Relationship with Yourself

If you are struggling with maintaining love banks, it could be because you first need to evaluate your personal love bank with yourself. One of the most frequently given advice about relationships is that we're not capable of really loving another person until we really love ourselves. We can't give away what we don't have. It goes beyond that, though. If we're going to focus on building relationships with others, our first order of business has to be our relationship with ourselves.

Our feelings about ourselves do have a significant influence on our feelings about others, and vice versa. If we dislike ourselves or feel unworthy, that interferes with relationship-building, especially in our romantic partnerships. People who have low self-esteem will underestimate how much their partner loves them—perhaps feeling like they are "undeserving" of that love. Because we manifest our own reality, the result is becoming less satisfied with the relationship and less optimistic about both the present and the potential future.

If you expect rejection, rejection will come, and if you're looking for signs your partner doesn't love or respect you, you're going to find them. Sometimes, it might really be happening. Other times, you may merely be misinterpreting. Either way, you've entered a vicious cycle: You feel bad about yourself and enter bad relationships. Those feelings of self-doubt are magnified and reinforced, and you lose sight of the fact that you deserve happiness. In the end, you are willing to tolerate mediocre treatment. So, for obvious reasons, high self-esteem is vital to a healthy relationship. (High self-esteem is not to be confused with narcissism, which can present as an inflated sense of self-importance and selfishness.)

You can and must foster your own self-esteem, but you've got to do it without losing sight of what others need. If you get too wrapped up in your ego, you run the risk of being willing to leave a relationship earlier than you should or simply giving up when problems arise, rather than taking constructive approaches to repair or strengthen your relationships. Pinning your level of self-esteem to your ego can make you fragile: you can quickly become overly dependent on other people to validate you. That type of foundation for your self-image is much more susceptible to cracks.

Self-love is essential to building relationships worthy of your deposits and investments, which begins with acceptance and authenticity. Be who you are, love who you are, love others the way you want to be loved, and translate that into receiving the love that you deserve.

Know When to Stop Depositing

On occasion, you will form relationships with people who cannot give you what you require, or people who expect something they can't give in return. It won't be long until those relationships are on life support, always teetering on the edge of a crash, requiring you to continually give it more and more. If a relationship is on life support, you must ask yourself, "Is this worth it to me? Is it worth the drama? Is it worth me continuing to watch the toxicity channel, or read the toxicity times?" If the answer is no, sometimes, you have to cancel those subscriptions.

It's a harsh fact of life, but not every friendship or business partnership or romantic relationship is meant to last forever. Sometimes, when they end, it can come with some heartbreak, but that's natural and normal, and winnowing down your relationship investment portfolio can be a good thing.

I'm not suggesting you start giving up on friendships quickly, and you indeed should not be ending partnerships that have brought you happiness and optimism over small disagreements. I am telling you that you can give yourself permission to take a failing relationship off life support. There may be friendships that once brought you joy but are now taking more from you than they give. You aren't required to maintain relationships with people whose paths diverge from yours—and you're not wrong if you choose to go another way. It is normal and natural to outgrow relationships, and that kind of growth should be welcomed.

How do you know when it's time to stop depositing in a relationship? If you've been making an effort to meet someone—whether that's at 50/50 or at 80/20—and you find yourself out on a limb alone, or if they're demanding more of your time and energy, both physical and emotional, than they're willing to give, well, that just might be a poor investment.

There are some typical signs of this happening. The idea of spending time with them can exhaust you. You may start ducking their calls or finding excuses not to make plans. When things bring joy into our lives and feed our optimism, we subconsciously gravitate toward them. We recognize when something makes us feel good, and we want more of it. If you're taking forever to answer texts from a specific person because you don't feel like having a conversation, that might be an indicator that it's time to stop depositing into that relationship.

When that time comes, be firm (and forthright) in your decision. Even if you're leaving a relationship, friendship, or partnership because that person isn't giving you what you need or deserve, you must continue treating them as you want to be treated. You have to keep on manifesting your reality by putting positivity out into the world.

When breaking up with a romantic partner, you need to just come out and say it. "Ghosting" a person may feel more trouble-free than having an awkward, tearful conversation, but it's really a selfish move that will only bring more anxiety and guilt into your life. What's the point, if you're making another suffer *and* not really missing out on the suffering yourself?

When it's a friend you're breaking up with, the slow fade might not be so bad. Don't ignore text messages or calls—that's just like ghosting. But the more you're unable to hang out, odds are, the more infrequently they will ask. At some point, they will get the message, and, honestly, if you were getting negativity out of the relationship, you likely weren't alone. They might be relieved, too.

Don't feel like you need to tell that friend why you're withdrawing your investment and choosing not to make any more deposits. In many cases, an explanation would simply increase the hurt. If you still want to try to fix the relationship and move forward, talking about it is not only healthy but also necessary. But, if you really are done, they don't really need to know why.

If you're attempting to taper off the relationship and they aren't getting the hint, it might be time for that super awkward conversation. Just be confident, firm, and kind as you explain that you've outgrown one another: things that make you feel less than favorable result in you giving back something less than positive.

In a relationship where neither person feels nurtured, no one is benefitting.

Monitor Your Emotional Bank Account

Just like you track your spending and receivables, it's important to be monitoring the deposits and withdrawals you're making in your relationships. There will be months (or years!) when you deposit in smaller amounts and withdraw quite a bit. At other times, you'll be depositing like crazy. Most deposits are the small acts you do to make people happy: the tiny, conscientious things, acts of physical affection, and kind words. What's important is that every so often, you take the time to check in on your emotional bank account balance.

It boils down to the same general point I discussed in the previous chapter, about unlocking your ability to empower yourself. You manifest your environment, and empowering yourself is what allows you to empower others. It's the same idea here: the love and positivity you receive are dependent on the love and positivity you put out into the world. Just like self-empowerment, making the correct deposits, investments, and withdrawals—and monitoring your emotional bank account—takes work. But, ultimately, the work becomes irrelevant when you find yourself manifesting optimism in your surroundings, environment, and relationships, and giving what you expect in return.

Forgiveness Relationship Response

Do not act like the sinful people of the world. Let God change your life. First of all, let Him give you a new mind. Then you will know what God wants you to do. And the things you do will be good and pleasing and perfect.

—Romans 12:2

Another way that you will have to be ready to give what you receive is related to the area of forgiveness. The truth is that living in the world can make it challenging to even want to forgive. In addition to COVID-19, a second "pandemic" of racial protest erupted when George Floyd, a resident of St. Louis Park, Minnesota, died on Monday, May 25, 2020, at the age of forty-six. Floyd was killed while in the custody of Minneapolis police officers, sparking nationwide protests against police brutality. Derek Chauvin, a white police officer, knelt on Floyd's neck for almost nine minutes while Floyd was handcuffed facedown in the street. Two other officers further restrained Floyd, and a fourth officer prevented onlookers from intervening. The raw and unfiltered video went viral and led to a racial awakening that caused global protest around the world. On June 18, 2020, *USA Today* reported that "There have been demonstrations in at least 1,700 places so far, large and small, across all 50 states."

The ongoing protests were also the result of other senseless, violent killings of black Americans: Ahmaud Arbery was killed in Georgia on February 23, 2020, just months before Floyd's murder. While jogging, Arbery was shot and killed after being pursued by white men who later said that they thought he was a burglary suspect. The video of Arbery's death was released on May 5.

The month following Arbery's death, on March 13, Officers Hankison, Mattingly, and Cosgrove entered Breonna Taylor's residence on a "no-knock" warrant in a drug investigation. Later reports discovered that the person the police were looking for did not live at Taylor's house and had been arrested shortly before. The officers blindly fired ten rounds into the apartment, killing Taylor. On June 19, 2020, news outlets covered a press conference announcing that Brett Hankison, one of three police officers involved in the March 13 shooting of Breonna Taylor, would be fired from the Louisville Metro Police Department according to Mayor Greg Fischer. At the time of this writing, there is a national outcry for justice for Taylor and her family, calling for the officers' arrests involved.

From March to June, the incidents of racial injustice and violence swelled daily and weekly news cycles on Memorial Day weekend as the video of George Floyd's death went viral. Another viral occurrence took place between Amy Cooper and Christian Cooper. Amy Cooper is a white New York woman who was recorded in a viral video calling the police and complaining that a black man was threatening her life. In actuality, he had merely asked her to leash her dog in the Ramble section of Central Park on Memorial Day. Not surprisingly, the incident on Monday, May 25, quickly spread on social media.

Days earlier, police in South Florida arrested and charged Patricia Ripley in the death of her nine-year-old special needs child Alejandro Ripley, who was autistic and nonverbal, after law enforcement officials said she falsely accused two black men of abducting her son. Miami-Dade County State Attorney Katherine Fernandez Rundle said that Ripley apparently tried to drown her son an hour earlier at a different canal at the Kendall Acres Condominium complex; however, nearby residents heard yelling and rescued him. Just an hour later, Ripley allegedly took Alejandro to a different canal, and this time, she took his life. Ripley's son was found floating in a canal near Miccosukee Golf and Country Club in Miami on May 22, 2020.

Black people are tired. Americans are tired. Generation Z (those born between 1996 and 2010) are engulfed with anger, and the protests rage on. As a matter of fact, there have been ongoing national protests since the murder of George Floyd. More recent incidents of violence in Portland, Oregon, and Kenosha, Wisconsin, are still unfolding as of September 2020.

The truth is that sometimes evil and inappropriate behavior can make you want to respond similarly. The longer I live, I am consistently baffled at just how horrific people treat each other. However, like the Romans scripture suggests: We can't respond to sin and evil deeds the way sinners do. At the end of the day, we must ask ourselves when something goes down, what is my response supposed to be? For starters, we must understand that if we want to be forgiven, we must forgive. That can be tough when the world is going crazy all around you.

Forgiveness Responses

I've drawn from the scriptures for insight into how to respond with forgiveness. I hope these words bring you comfort and empower you to move past your grievances with grace.

To respond to an insult:

> **11** *Blessed are you when people insult you, persecute you and falsely say all kinds of evil against you because of me.*
> **12** *Rejoice and be glad, because great is your reward in heaven, for in the same way they persecuted the prophets who were before you.... Make a choice to rejoice; think of it as earning bonus points on your way to heaven.*
>
> —Matthew 5:11–12

To respond when you are angry:

> **26** *In your anger, do not sin:*
> *Do not let the sun go down while you are still angry,*
> **27** *and do not give the devil a foothold.*
>
> —Ephesians 4:26–27

Anger is not an excuse for sin, and you should make a point to release anger quickly so that the rage doesn't build up inside of you. Take heart in these words:

> **18** *If it is possible, as far as it depends on you,*
> *live at peace with everyone.* **19** *Do not take revenge,*
> *my dear friends, but leave room for God's wrath,*
> *for it is written: "It is mine to avenge; I will repay,"*
> *says the Lord.* **20** *On the contrary: "If your enemy*
> *is hungry, feed him; if he is thirsty, give him*
> *something to drink. In doing this, you will*
> *heap burning coals on his head."*
>
> —Romans 12:18–20

When you face enemies, the Bible instructs you to:

1. Try your best to live at peace with everyone.

2. Do not attempt revenge on your own; leave your haters in God's hands.

3. Instead of striking out against them in anger, actually show acts of kindness while you wait for God to avenge you.

How to Apply Forgiveness

> *"Start with the people who never apologized to you,*
> *release their power over your heart."*
>
> —KSR

The first step of forgiveness is *what you say* when you are angry. Here a few inappropriate responses:

I will never forgive them for that.
They don't deserve to be forgiven.
I just don't think I will be able to get over it.

What is the appropriate response? As Jesus said:

> *"Father, forgive them, for they do not*
> *know what they are doing."*
>
> —Luke 23:34

Forgive them; they know not what they do. Not everyone who causes you harm intentionally means to hurt you. The story of Joseph is a powerful one of forgiveness. After his brothers sold him into slavery, Joseph experienced many trials, but ultimately, he ended up being promoted to number two, second only to Pharaoh. While there was a famine going on in the rest of the region, Joseph's management of the resources put him in a prime position to provide food and resources to the same family that had sold him into slavery. Instead of focusing on the pain they caused him, Joseph has one of the best forgiveness responses ever! He said:

> *You intended to harm me, but God intended*
> *it for good to accomplish what is now being done,*
> *the saving of many lives.*
>
> —Genesis 50:20

This means that even though Joseph's enemies intended him harm, God caused their actions to work out in his favor. And that will happen for us as well; we just have to be prepared to give the forgiveness we want to receive.

Forgiving Is Not Forgetting

Forgiving is not the same as forgetting. There are some offenses that can be done to you where forgiveness can be applied, but forgetting is not required. If you are injured or abused physically, emotionally, psychologically, or mentally by someone, you have a right to protect yourself from further harm. Just because you make the decision to forgive someone doesn't mean that they should be allowed in your inner circle or have an active role in your life.

Exercise: Reflecting on Your Relationships

Spend some time in quiet contemplation with your journal or notebook as you respond to the following prompts:

- Have you taken someone for granted?

- Does the saying, "You don't know what you've got until it's gone" apply to you? If so, how?

- How easy are you to get along with?

- What are some things you need to do to improve your relationships with people?

- Is your goal to connect deeply or superficially with others?

- If an important relationship or friendship ended because you hurt the other person, apologize. If you want this relationship back in your life, write about how you will try to repair it.

- When an opportunity for a new romantic relationship or friendship presents itself, what will you do differently following this reflective journey? What negative traits are you willing to leave behind?

Chapter 8

DISCOURAGEMENT ELIMINATOR 8:
Master the Art of Becoming a
Chameleon

THERE IS A TON of research out there about what it takes to change minds and influence people, but one thing is for sure: our tendency is to trust, follow, and respect the people we like, and, by and large, the people we find most harmonious are the people we think are most like us. Some people are more attuned to this than others and make it a point to tweak their personalities depending on their environment and the people they are with to make the best possible impression. These folks can be thought of as "chameleons," after the lizard that can change its color and pattern, sometimes to camouflage itself. Being a human chameleon often gets a bad rap, but let go of that preconception and learn how you can get the best out of situations by adopting this art. When you get the best out of situations, your optimism levels will skyrocket.

Social Chameleons

Mark Snyder, a social psychologist at the University of Minnesota in the 1980s, studied social chameleons and their near-pathological ability to shift their personality traits to make the best possible impression. They always "try to be the right person in the right place at the right time," Mark Snyder told Daniel Goleman of the *New York Times* in 1985. "They continually monitor their social performance, skillfully adjusting it when they detect that they are not having the desired effect."

Most of us are either social chameleons or their opposite: zebras. A zebra can't change its stripes. Dr. Snyder's research referred to chameleons and zebras as high self-monitors and low self-monitors. Self-monitoring refers to the ability or the tendency to critique, or at least pay attention to, one's own behavior during interactions. In summary, he found that high self-monitors, or social chameleons, tended to have a few traits in common:

"They pay careful attention to social cues, scrutinizing others with keenness to know what is expected of them before making a response.

"In order to get along and to be liked, they try to be as others expect them to be. For example, they try to make people they dislike think they are friendly with them.

"They use their social abilities to mold their appearance as different situations demand, so that, as some put it, 'With different people, I act like a very different person.'...

"By contrast, those low in self-monitoring subscribe to the credo, 'To thine own self be true.' They feel it is more important to act in accord with one's values, no matter the social consequences."

Another researcher at the University of Minnesota, Christopher Leone, found that children develop either chameleon-like or zebra-like personality traits as early as elementary school. In Leone's experiment, researchers asked third graders about their opinions on several topics. Before they gave their answers, the children were allowed to see other children's responses. Some decided to look closely at that information before giving their own answer. Others were deemed most likely to become social chameleons, due to the fact that one of the self-monitoring hallmarks include finding ways to get other people's preferences and opinions before choosing their own choices and opinions.

How Can Being a Chameleon Benefit You?

Being a chameleon can be a huge benefit, particularly when it comes to making friends and influencing people. Critics will call a chameleon "fake" because they act in a way that mirrors or complements the people around them. But there's a significant difference between being "fake" and knowing how to adapt to a situation to best serve your own needs and make the people around you feel as comfortable as possible.

Some career paths are natural choices for chameleons. These are jobs that bring success to people who can carefully craft the impression they make. Trial lawyers are a great example. While it takes an enormous amount of skill and knowledge to be marginally successful, the best of the best have a particular secret weapon that they whip out when they get in front of a jury. The secret weapon is their chameleon-like nature and the ability to morph into precisely the person who's going to best get through to the jury members.

That's just one example—the same is true of actors, politicians, and even salespeople. It's true of the people you knew in high school or college who seemed to be equally at home with the jocks, the sorority sisters, and the academics. It's also true of me. I've worked very hard to get where I am professionally, but what's undoubtedly helped has been my ability to fit in with any group of people.

It may be helpful to understand temperaments before we continue. The foundation of four basic temperaments was conceived by Hippocrates centuries ago. Hippocrates' temperament theory divides all people into four basic categories. Let's take a look at each.

Sanguine

Extroverted, spirited sanguine types are earnest, joyful, lively, and fun-loving. This temperament is receptive by nature, and their infectious energy generally brightens the path of everyone they interact with, transferring their friendly, outgoing persona.

Strengths: Loves life, compassionate, optimistic, friendly

Weaknesses: Restless, undisciplined, egotistical, emotional

Professions: Salespeople, politicians, actors, speakers, lawyers

Phlegmatic

Introverted, peacemaking phlegmatic types are typically loyal and tend to avoid conflict at all costs. They always try to mediate between others to create serenity and harmony. They are very giving and love helping others.

Strengths: Easygoing, likable, practical, dependable

Weaknesses: Unmotivated, stubborn, indecisive, fearful

Professions: Nursing, social workers, accountants, teachers, technicians, diplomats

Choleric

Goal-oriented choleric types are savvy, analytical, and logical. They are typically practical and straightforward.

Strengths: Courageous, self-confident, strong-willed, determined, independent

Weaknesses: Unsympathetic, inconsiderate, unforgiving, domineering, opinionated, crafty

Professions: Leaders, producers, builders, statisticians, programmers

Melancholic

Detail-oriented, gifted, idealists, melancholic types are very social and seek to contribute to the community. These individuals are extremely thorough, accurate, and meticulous.

Strengths: Self-disciplined, loyal, conscientious, self-sacrificing

Weaknesses: Moody, negative, critical, revengeful, impractical, rigid, persecution prone

Professions: Artists, musicians, inventors, philosophers, doctors

If you are curious about your primary temperament, I encourage you to explore the topic deeper. There are many online tests that allow you to discover your primary temperament, and others that also explain your personality blend or mix. These mixes provide both a primary and secondary personality type, although you may have been able to pick yours out from just the short descriptions provided.

The more you learn about yourself, the more you know how to morph into who you need to be in any given situation. Being a chameleon, though, isn't about changing who you are. That's the most important thing to remember as you develop this skill. An actual chameleon is always a chameleon—it is not capable of shape-shifting into another creature altogether. A chameleon changes specific characteristics (in this case, its skin color) to fit its environment. It never stops being chameleon-shaped; it just blends in a little better. If you feel like you need to change who you are as a person to be successful or to be accepted, you're doing it wrong, and that will ultimately negatively impact your self-image and, in turn, your self-empowerment. What I am talking about is developing the ability to highlight aspects of your personality that help you adapt to your environment and the people in it, while always—always—staying true to yourself.

To become a capable social and professional chameleon, you first need to have a firm grasp of your personality's significant aspects (review the four basic temperaments again). Once you've gotten to know yourself really well, you'll understand all the different people who make up the authentic, whole, and beautiful you. Then, you can quickly determine which of those personality aspects should take the lead in different situations—professional, personal, and social—that you find yourself in.

What Kind of Self-Monitoring Are You Doing?

The first step to getting to know yourself this way is figuring out whether you're a natural chameleon or a natural zebra. If your personality is consistent, regardless of the situation you're in or the people you're interacting with, you're a zebra. (And remember, a zebra doesn't change its stripes!)

Zebras are called low self-monitors, and they focus much less on self-presentation, displaying their unchanging, singular personality at all times. There's no shame in the zebra game: it is delightful to be so confident in who you are that you never waver. But the drawback to being a zebra is that you will undoubtedly encounter situations and people who don't totally vibe with you. They may not recognize themselves or their own characteristics in you, and they may be under the almost certainly mistaken impression that you don't have anything in common. Even if they're wrong, the end result is that you'll be less able to influence or lead people who don't see themselves in you and therefore innately like you. So, even if you're a natural zebra, and proud of it, it's worthwhile to learn some of the skills a chameleon uses to get ahead.

Chameleons are, perhaps unsurprisingly, high self-monitors. They're driven by the desire to fit in and be accepted, and they reap the benefits of near-constant likeability in both business and social arenas. They develop a set of social skills, including the ability to "read" people using cues, characteristics, and emotions, and then alter their own emotional expressions and behaviors to reflect or complement the ones they're seeing.

Fit in to Get Ahead

High self-monitors often find it easier to get along with a wide range of people and personality types, making them more likely to end up in leadership positions, have bigger networks, and even go on more dates. Research shows that chameleons are more likely to be asked for help; in a work environment, being asked for assistance and coming through for people can be the quickest way to impress people and get ahead.

In a 2016 study published in the journal *Organization Science*, Professor Blaine Landis of the University College of London School of Management wrote, "This position as an informal advisor was found to be more closely tied to job performance and career success than other positions within the [professional] network. Claiming more ties to other people—i.e., saying that many people are your friends—isn't correlated with success, it's having other people claim ties to you."

Chameleons in the workplace, or anywhere, don't necessarily have more friends. What they *do* have is more people who *claim them* as friends. Being a chameleon is different from being merely agreeable: people who are too amenable may let their opinions be too easily swayed. This makes them a lot less dependable for advice and keeps them from reaping the benefits of being some-one's go-to person in the office.

Being the chameleon makes you more than likable—it makes people see you as dependable. One of the best ways to get ahead in your career is to be always ready to help and offer valuable advice and opinions to as many people as possible.

Of course, there can be drawbacks to being the chameleon, both for other people and for you. If other people realize you're adapt-ing to your environment, highlighting different aspects of your personality at varying times, they may believe you're a "phony." A high self-monitor is driven by a desire to—and the value of—fitting in. However, that can slip too far to one extreme, and lead a chameleon to follow the crowd and lose sight of themselves.

Get to Know Your Many Facets

Chameleons tend to have significant personality components that come out in various environments of their lives. At work, you may have one persona—the professional, advice-giving mentor. When you're with your friends, perhaps you have several: the fun-loving partier or the dependable shoulder to cry on. When you're with your family, you may have yet another persona (and odds are, that's the *most* authentic version, though it is not necessarily your favorite).

Those personas—and how often you switch them—will almost certainly change as you gain life experience. In my thirties, I was everything I pretended to be, embodying the phrase, "Fake it till you make it." It did serve me well to hone my skill at adapting to my surroundings, but I wasn't always entirely comfortable. I would find myself trying to please everyone and, in turn, attempt to be a person I knew I honestly was not. By the time I reached my forties, I had gained a measure of comfort with myself I couldn't have imagined at twenty-five or even thirty-five.

You have to understand and know your value and self-worth in this game of optimism and life. You can't play if you don't know who you are. There were times where my goal was to keep up with the Joneses; now I realize the real mentality of success requires you to internalize that we—you and me—*we are the Joneses.*

I'm still a chameleon, but I never, ever compromise who I truly am. There are different versions and personas inside me, sure, but I love every one of them, and I *need* every one of them to be the successful, optimistic woman I am. Sometimes, I am Kimmie. She's your girlfriend, the fun one who will kick it with you on Saturday night. In fact, most of my girlfriends do call me Kimmie. She's the part of me who laughs really loud and eats hot wings. She's someone a lot of people who know me in other contexts—mostly the professional ones—don't realize exists.

I love Kimmie deeply. She's responsible for many of the most fun moments in my life, and she's fantastic because she's fearless. She got that way thanks to my parents, who raised me to be brave, to embrace fun, and to believe when I was five years old that there is magic and wonder in the world, and that it's okay to be expressive about the joy those things bring to your life. More importantly, Kimmie is beautiful and confident because my dad told me every day how beautiful and brave I was. Kimmie is who I am when I'm alone with myself.

Kimmie is an essential and beloved part of who I am, but those are also the aspects of my personality I most need to keep in check in other circumstances. I cannot be Kimmie in the boardroom. I cannot be that version of me at my women's organizational meetings. I cannot be Kimmie with some women who believe they have *arrived*, and that they're better than Kimmie. That last part isn't a reflection of me and who I am: it's just the insecurity of women still learning to stand in their own power.

The businesswoman in me is "Kimberly S. Reed," who is the entrepreneur and the businesswoman. She is all things professional, all things education. She means business. Kimberly S. Reed is the version of me who *is* accepted by those women who have arrived. My upbringing helped shape her, too. I grew up in a place where I was privileged, with two college-educated parents. They took exceptional care of me and ensured that I had every advantage regarding my education, both academically and socially. Kimberly S. Reed is accepted in places where Kimmie would never be welcomed. She's powerful enough that some men find her intimidating.

It's Kimberly S. Reed who has developed a distinguished

reputation as having one of the most distinct and influential voices on the lecture circuit, and who has transformed the thinking of thousands. Kimberly is a regularly invited speaker and lecturer at the Wharton School of the University of Pennsylvania LEAD Program, National Leadership Consortium, Temple University, KPMG, and Howard University Leadership Programs and the conferences of leading national professional organizations. She's the expert in me, who has been a respected leader and guide for some of the world's most influential companies' global diversity, equality and inclusion strategies.

Then, independent of those two women, there's Kim. Kim's the middle-of-the-road version of my identity, who's comfortable at conferences and chatting in line at the grocery store. She's the version of me my friends look to when they need advice or a shoulder to lean on.

All of these women are beautiful, and without any one of them, I can't be who I am. Remember, even when we're talking about adapting to different people and situations, your first priority always has to be maintaining your own authenticity.

Be a Chameleon without Losing Yourself

I've always had a strong personality. As a kid, I was called "bubbly" or "outgoing." As a grown woman, I have become known for my infectious energy, lioness tone, and inspiring sincerity.

I am capable of inspiring confidence in people because I am confident in myself; this all goes back to the central idea that you can't do anything for other people until you get right with yourself. You can only empower others if you are confident and sure. And you can only inspire confidence and optimism in others as long as you are fully vested in yourself, your purpose, and your abilities.

Of course, most of us struggle with seasons of insecurity. Even if we manage to adopt a persona of confidence, we can privately struggle with not fully knowing ourselves or not feeling like we can indeed *be* ourselves. As we grow more confident and more able to maintain all the aspects of ourselves and simply highlight individual personas for specific environments and circumstances, that self-criticism can morph into self-reflection. That's how you get to know yourself. That's how I came to know and love Kimmie, Kimberly S. Reed, and Kim. That's how I grew my confidence and optimism, and that has made all the difference in propelling me forward in my professional and personal life.

You don't have to become a new person. To effectively use the skills of a chameleon, you just have to get to know who you already are. As you gain experience and understanding, you grow into your true self—and that's made up of all these different people.

So, how do you become a chameleon without losing yourself? There are many ways to practice the art of reading people and shifting just a bit in your skin to better fit the circumstances:

- Study people whose personalities you admire: What it is about them that you want to emulate? How can you interpret those personality traits and make them part of who you are?

- Put yourself into unfamiliar situations. It may feel risky, but with high risk comes high reward. The more new situations and environments you put yourself in and the more new people you interact with, the more effective your self-discovery will be. Pay attention to how you respond to new things you like, and, just as important, new things you don't. That's how you'll learn where you really stand.

- Most important, understand that there's never a good reason to *hide* part of who you are. When I'm meeting with the CEOs of Fortune 500 companies, Kimberly S. Reed is behind the wheel. But that doesn't mean Kim and Kimmie aren't still in the car. I can't be any of these women without the two others, and I wish more people understood that.

You have to be true to yourself, even if that means feeling like you're multiple people. Each of those personalities will be a perfect fit at their own time. When you walk into a room, you instinctively must know when to turn it on and off and its uniqueness. Being a chameleon never changes who you are—just teaches you to adapt to the environment. I'm always going to be these three women. I just know which of them belong where.

The most useful thing about the idea that some of us are chameleons and some of us are zebras is understanding the difference between high self-monitors and low self-monitors. It is essential to understand that these different personality types exist. Acknowledging the differences—and the fact that both personality types have benefits and detriments—can help you hone your sense of self and ensure that any self-critiquing you do is constructive. Knowing how to strategically deploy the skills of a chameleon can help you get ahead professionally, and, more personally, it will probably make more people like you. But keep just a little bit of that zebra in your heart, and you'll ensure that you never forget who you are. It's important to be liked, but it's more important to like yourself.

Exercise: Who Are You?

Set aside some time for yourself, and with your journal or notebook in hand, respond to the following prompts:

- Do you tend toward being more like a chameleon or more like a zebra?

- If you identify as a zebra, are you willing to adopt some chameleon-like qualities to better inspire and lead others?

- Referring to the descriptions in this chapter, which of the four basic temperament do you think describes you the most? If you took an online temperament test, what was your result? Do you agree or disagree? Why?

- Describe who you are with your friends, with your family, in professional settings, and other situations. Do you have different names for these versions of yourself, like I do?

- Are you willing to experiment with a new style of approaching situations? What is something new you can try without holding back? Write about what you plan to do.

- Write about the extraordinary person you are. Describe your internal and external beauty in your own words. What about your beauty is unique and original?

● ●

Chapter 9

DISCOURAGEMENT ELIMINATOR 9:
Use the Power of Your
Rearview

HAVE YOU EVER NOTICED the tiny message printed on your car's mirrors: OBJECTS IN THE MIRROR ARE CLOSER THAN THEY APPEAR? I have a message to share with you along those lines: LIFE'S SEASONS ARE CLOSER THAN THEY APPEAR. You can be moving right along, feeling like things are going smoothly and then, in the blink of an eye, find yourself in life's darkest moments. Before you know it, you're knee-deep in pain and grief.

The good news is that this is a truth that works in the other direction, too. Why do you think the rearview mirror is smaller than your windshield? We are supposed to spend less time looking in the past, and more time looking ahead! When you're in the midst of that terrible season, it's easy to forget that age-old wisdom, that this, too, shall pass. Usually, you can be sure it will pass sooner than you think it possibly could. While grief and mourning can be a state that lasts your whole life, the acute pain often fades quickly enough that you don't even realize it has subsided until you take a look in the rearview. And that's a valuable—and healthy—thing to do.

Without the Darkness, You Will Not Recognize the Light

In the days, weeks, and months after my mom and grandmother passed away, while I was being diagnosed and battling my own cancer, the passage of time seemed to warp. Some days stretched on forever. Other times, it felt like I had lost whole weeks. Even now, it sometimes feels like no time has passed since that dark season of my life, although it's years in my rearview.

We all know it isn't healthy to dwell in the past. You can get caught in a loop, replaying the things that have hurt you repeatedly and trying to find some new bit of information or explanation that simply doesn't exist. No one ever found healing by living their life in the past, but only thinking about the future can present its own problems, too. That is an excellent way to get wrapped up in anxiety and find you paralyzed, unable to really move forward. The way forward through hardship and pain is to focus on the present and take things one day at a time, trying to live fully in the moment. So, how do you manage to savor the present, move toward the future, and honor the past without getting stuck in it?

The secret is to glance in the rearview. Where you are going is almost entirely informed by and dependent on where you've been. Therefore, it is important to remind yourself of that fact. By glancing in the rearview, you not only remind yourself of where you started and of the experiences that have shaped you up until this point, but you may also be surprised at how far you've come from that darkest point.

Darkness is an unfortunate reality of life. I was lucky and, all things considered, I did not face a whole lot of darkness for the first decades of my life. Once I did encounter life's hard truths, though, it was through one cruel twist of fate after another. My mother and grandmother died of cancer, and then I battled my own cancer without the two women who had been there for me through every other season in my life.

You can work to embrace the darkness with gratitude. Maybe that sounds crazy. Perhaps you're thinking, *How could you ever be grateful for such horrible tragedies?* But it's possible to be grateful for even the harsh, seemingly unbearable occurrences in your life because they become the low moments against which you're able to better appreciate the highs. Every journey will have peaks and valleys, and that is a beautiful thing because one allows you to appreciate the other. The most beautiful, awe-inspiring mountains simply can't exist without the valleys between them. In short, you can't have one without the other, and so to indeed come to appreciate the light, you have to know what it's like to have lived in the dark.

Your darkest seasons can put you on the road toward the light. The difficult seasons of life do more than instill in us an appreciation for the simple, joyful ones. They can also help us get there. Once you have carried yourself through what feels like the most terrible days of your life, you will have a new benchmark for how strong and capable you actually are. Optimism can carry you through the dark. Once you know what types of storms you can weather, life's struggles begin to feel less insurmountable. Don't misunderstand me: I am not suggesting optimism will make your losses less painful. They will still hurt. But a glance in your rearview, at what you have already come through and survived, will remind you that things do get more manageable and that you are strong enough to continue down the road.

How to Look at the Rearview

I've been speaking mostly in metaphors, but there are concrete, actionable ways to examine what's in your rearview. One of the easiest ways is to keep a physical record of your challenges and losses and your wins—the big and the small—that ultimately highlights the victories in your life. Another way is to mentally reflect on them. Let's look at both approaches:

- **Track Your Actions**. One of the easiest ways to look in your "review mirror" is to keep a journal or a daily "done" list. This method offers you two separate but related benefits: First, it helps you accomplish things by giving you a rush of dopamine (the hormone most closely associated with happiness) every time you add something to the list. You will find you have the impetus to do much more when each thing you accomplish makes you just a little bit happier. The second benefit is that it serves as a reminder of how much you have accomplished. Later, when you feel like you are not being productive enough or won't be able to accomplish everything on your to-do list, simply flip through the "done" lists and marvel at everything you have been able to do to complete and achieve.

- **Meditate and Reflect.** Set aside some time for deliberate, focused reflection; think of it almost like a meditation. Focus on a memory from your past. This could be a few weeks, a semester of your academic career, a year, or even a decade of your life. Consider all the milestones that came along throughout that period. You've probably been through graduations, relationships, breakups, holidays, promotions, firings, hirings, and other meaningful moments. Think of this as a virtual flip-book that reflects your growth. Every one of these critical moments— whether they were failures or successes, has brought you to a new place in your journey, and has taught you valuable lessons. (Whenever you do this exercise, try to choose a different period in your past.)

Each season of life brings us new challenges and lessons. In adolescence, we learn to connect with others, begin lifelong friendships, and develop precious inner emotional experiences that will ultimately shape who we become. Our teen years are when we wrestle with first loves and, almost inevitably, first heartbreaks. As young adults, we strike out on our own, trying in equal measure to depend on ourselves and be self-sufficient, and to hang on to the family connections that have been such a vital part of our support system.

Even if all those lessons are so far in your rearview that you have to squint to see them, they are just as relevant now as they were back then. Everything is relative: at the time, the challenges you faced seemed enormous, and so did the victories. Just because your adolescent worries seem silly to the adult version of yourself doesn't invalidate them. It has taken every experience, every loss, and every win to get you here and make you into the beautiful, strong, optimistic person you are.

For me, the decades following adolescence were the most challenging. I knew what I wanted professionally. My personality, network-building abilities, and willingness to embrace an unceasing hustle helped me manifest every magnificent thing I wished for myself in my career. But at the height of my success, I lost my two closest confidants—my mother and grandmother—and then got a good long look at the reality of my own mortality with my cancer diagnosis and treatment.

As you reflect on your past, you must not skip the sad stuff. It's possible to draw optimism from even the most negative memories in your rearview. The losses that have marked us the most are the ones with the most precise ability to empower us. Don't tuck those dark moments away: drag them out into the sun. Your perseverance through those times represents your most significant victories of all. If you hide them away, they cease to be victories. If you occasionally drag them out, as painful as they are, and wear them like a badge of honor, they give you power.

You are not defined by the worst things that have happened to you. You are not defined by your failings or by the bad choices you've made. You are not defined by the tragedies that have befallen you. Do not let the fear of reliving these moments keep you from reflecting on them and gleaning the lessons they offer.

I think about the last forty-five days of my mom's life almost every day. In the first months after she died, all those horrible moments played in a painful loop in my head. There was nothing helpful about that. With that traumatic season of life in my rearview, I can revisit who I was in those days, and see clearly how I was honed—sharpened in some ways, softened in others—by having gone through that and come out the other side.

Help Someone with Their Rearview

When someone you know is going through a difficult time, you can help them by taking a quiet moment to recall a similar struggle in your own rearview. Use your fresh perspective, aided by the insight you have gained with time, to offer them real understanding and to help them keep moving forward.

Your rearview reminds you what you've been through, and can smooth the road ahead, and you can use the past without living in it. I am despondent every day about the loss of my mom and grandmother. Would I change my path to have more time with them? Of course, in a heartbeat. But I understand that living through their loss, everything that came before, and indeed what came after helps me help others and is what made me the unflagging optimist I am today.

Allow the Past to Empower Your Future

Imagine you are on a road trip, driving across the Great Plains. For long, lonely stretches, the landscape around you may look exactly the same. It's so monotonous, flat, and monochromatic, you can feel like you've driven for hours without going anywhere. A quick glance in the rearview mirror allows you to see just how far you have come. It is the perfect metaphor for life—especially the periods after our significant losses, failures, or shifts. We stare out at the long and winding road ahead, feeling like we've been traveling forever and wondering if we've even made any progress.

I opened the chapter with this statement, but it bears repeating: life's seasons are much closer than they appear. A glance in your rearview can make you all the more powerful. When you look in your rearview and see all you have been through, it gives you a sense of gratefulness and profound gratitude. It also gives you the strength to navigate any uncertain terrain ahead.

Let your past struggles remind you of your strength today. You will not know what you are capable of in the future unless you face adversity. In your life, there may be more moments of failure and defeat than a celebration. Or the number of triumphs may outweigh the number of frustrations and losses. Either way, use your rearview to remind you of your strength, tenacity, and the lessons you have learned to continue to walk through life's triumphs and valleys. Your rearview not only details all you have come through but also gives you the power to see how it can be used to accomplish your purpose in life when you are willing.

Exercise: What's in Your Rearview?

In addition to trying one or both of the methods under "How to Look at the Rearview" on page 134, contemplate the following questions and respond in your journal or notebook.

- What has distracted you in the past from being your best? Moving forward, how can you avoid similar distractions?

- What mistakes have you made as a result of not having all the information you needed? Have you been beating yourself up for those mistakes? Are you willing to give yourself a break for what you didn't know and practice being kinder to yourself? If so, how?

- What have you had to start over in your life? How did you feel about starting over? Was it a relief or was it difficult?

- With regard to racial equality, in what ways have you been too hard on yourself or others? How can you be more loving? What has the past taught you about your power and strength?

- With regard to religious freedom, in what ways have you been too hard on yourself or others? How can you be more loving? What has the past taught you about your power and strength?

- Having lived through a global pandemic, how have you changed? Do you look at yourself differently now? Are you in a better or worse place? Why? What can you do to make necessary changes? What good things have been added to your life as a result of this experience?

Chapter 10

DISCOURAGEMENT ELIMINATOR 10:
Take the Elevator to the "Executive"
Level

AS WE TAKE THIS FINAL TREK toward moving from defeat to life's C-suite, I trust that you have learned something transformative and helpful. I want to give you some final keys to establishing an optimism habit as a way of life. Adhering to these principles will support you through any difficult seasons you encounter.

A Higher Power Is Essential

To reach life's C-suite, it is essential to believe in a high power —that is, a being or energy, such as God, that has the power to affect nature and lives. I eventually found my way back to Christianity, but others may identify with a different higher power. For example, Anna Mae Bullock (better known as Tina Turner) was raised Baptist but became an adherent of Buddhism in the early seventies, making her higher power Buddha. Someone else's higher power may be Mother Nature or the Great Spirit or the Goddess or the Universe or All That Is or Spirit...the list goes on. Regardless of your "what" or "who," to remain hopeful and optimistic in the midst of life's storms, you need to trust in a power greater than yourself.

I am learning that trusting God and faith in God is not about a moment—it's about a lifetime. It is about a track record of seeing God come through in the past. Seeing God honor His word in my life, even amid disappointment, gives me faith that He can do it again. My hope is renewed. My trust in God is based on His Word and His faithfulness to perform His Promises. Jeremiah tells us that God watches over His word and is faithful to perform it. In the Bible, it reads:

> **12** *Then the Lord said to me,*
> *"You have seen well, for I am [actively]*
> *watching over My word to fulfill it."*
> —Jeremiah 1:12 (AMP)

That is certainly my testimony. Time and time again, I have seen God come through for me in impossible-looking situations, and the Bible tells me that He doesn't change:

Jesus Christ is [eternally changeless, always]
the same yesterday and today and forever.

—Hebrews 13:8

Moments of adverse reports or negative situations do not change the nature of God or His ability to redeem any situation in my life. So, in tough times, I have learned to remind myself that if God healed, delivered, or redeemed me in the past, then He is well able to do it again.

I encourage you to find this type of faith in your higher power by looking for supporting evidence and testimony. If you seek clues, you will find them. Why is faith in your higher power so important? Because it is *the* link to happiness.

Many of us have read countless articles and books on how to be happier, but we are not becoming the extraordinarily joyous people we hoped to be. Who could blame us for our frustration? The benefits of happiness are undeniable. It can help you live a longer, healthier life. But the truth is, many people have no idea how to *become* happier. They have lost sight of their faith in something greater than themselves. In fact, some people's pursuits of happiness backfire, causing them to end up more miserable than ever. I see this play across social media channels every day, especially with chronic selfie-takers and posters. There is nothing wrong with self-love, but often those pictures and posts camouflage a painful reality. We must be careful not to let our obsession with happiness prevent us from inevitability dealing with pain.

For a Full Life, Pain Is Necessary

The biggest misconception about happiness is that the path to achieving it involves *avoiding pain*. But pain is actually a necessary part of happiness, and research shows that it can lead to pleasure in several ways:

- **Pain helps you recognize pleasure.** If you felt happy all the time, you wouldn't recognize it as happiness. You need to experience the opposite end of the spectrum sometimes to be able to truly understand and appreciate joy.

- **Pain forms social bonds.** You likely relate to other people more easily when you have endured similar painful events in your life because pain promotes empathy, which is essential to social connection. The bonding caused by pain even increases cooperation and care among people. Volunteers often come together to clean up after a natural disaster or a charity that supports chronic illnesses because they experienced pain and loss and witnessed suffering. Remember the ice bucket challenge? Did you dump a cold bucket of water on yourself and post it on social media? I did not, but I donated instead. I had a lot of questions about the point of the cold water and the terror on people's faces. But I digress, the people who did do felt a bond and connection by that specific experience.

- **Pain gives you permission to reward yourself.** There is a reason a glass of wine tastes better after you have completed eighteen loads of laundry or a hot chocolate tastes better after you shovel yourself out of the driveway. Enduring pain actually makes you enjoy your rewards more. When you have worked out or completed some other difficult task, you are more likely to give yourself permission to enjoy a benefit. Not only will you then feel less guilt over splurging, but your senses will also be heightened, and you will actually appreciate the reward more.

Optimism Takes Commitment and Practice

Once I learned to trust in a power higher than myself, developed a healthy relationship with happiness, and understood that I would face pain, I was ready to fully embrace my life's C-suite by adopting optimism as a lifestyle. Regularly practicing the habits of optimism can help you create a peaceful, joyful life. There will still be times when certain situations and circumstances just don't make sense. In times like these, we need to draw more deeply on our faith in our higher power *and* put in more work to maintain our habits of optimism.

There's no quick fix to becoming a lifelong optimist other than possessing a willingness to work at it—from the moment you wake up in the morning until you close your eyes at night. You cannot magically wish yourself into optimism. It is a skill, and one you can never really stop practicing. You must be prepared to do three things:

1. Commit to optimism. Research says it takes a minimum of twenty-one days to form a new habit and thirty to sixty days to make that habit stick.

2. Shift your mindset and perspective to think positively. As you encounter things in life that discourage you from remaining hopeful and positive, eliminate them as you've learned to do throughout this book. If you focus on karate-chopping negative, vile, impure thoughts from your mind as soon as you have them, you will be on the path of positivity. Follow the divine recipe for optimism: Think pure thoughts, lovely thoughts, admirable thoughts, excellent thoughts, and praiseworthy thoughts. As Philippians 4:8–9 (NIV) states:

"Finally, brothers and sisters, whatever is true, whatever is noble, whatever is right, whatever is pure, whatever is lovely, whatever is admirable—if anything is excellent or praiseworthy—think about such things. Whatever you have learned or received or heard from me, or seen in me—put it into practice. And the God of peace will be with you."

3. Learn from other people's positive, life-affirming actions, and put those actions into practice in your own life.

Exercise: Faith and Commitment

Set aside some quiet time in a private space for yourself. In your journal or notebook, respond to the following prompts:

• Who or what do you consider your higher power? In what ways has your higher power acted in your life?

• What is your level of faith in your higher power? In what ways has your higher power come through for you? What steps can you take to deepen your faith?

• In what ways have painful life experiences taught you to appreciate life more fully?

• Write a commitment to yourself to practice being optimistic from the time you wake up in the morning until the time you go to bed. What are some of the things you will do throughout the day to stay on target?

CONCLUSION

CONGRATULATIONS on reaching the end of this book. I bet you are feeling more optimistic already! You are also probably realizing that it takes effort to look on the bright side. Even if you have been working at it for a long time, being optimistic is not always easy. There are still occasions when I genuinely don't feel like an optimist. But, truthfully, I have been working at this way of life for so long that my optimism has become a habit. Even if I'm feeling less than optimistic about something, I quickly default to feeling hopeful and positive about the future.

The tools and the encouragement in this book are designed to help you develop the mental and emotional fortitude to face every area of your life with optimism. As I've tried to impress upon you, there are seasons in all of our lives when we face challenges that seem too great to conquer. However, it is precisely when we are experiencing these life knockouts that we need to get back in the ring and fight.

Everyone's fight is going to be different, though there may be similarities. Cancer is one example that many can relate to. Although we live in an age of incredible medical and technological advances, the statistics of those being diagnosed with and battling cancer are staggering. Cancer is an epidemic in the United States, and breast cancer is a severe opponent for women. When it comes to cancer's ability to suck every bit of optimism from a patient and those who love them, I got more of a firsthand look than I could have bargained for. And I am not alone. According to the Susan G. Komen Foundation, in 2020, it is estimated that among women in the United States there will be:

- 276,480 *new* cases of invasive breast cancer (not recurrences of original breast cancers)
- 48,530 new cases of ductal carcinoma in situ (DCIS), a non-invasive breast cancer
- 42,170 breast cancer deaths

Even with all the advances in medicine and technology, people are still in a medical crisis. Yet, there is hope in the middle of the fight. Like those I have shared with you, practical tools and tactics will aid in the battle against pervasive pessimism.

An optimistic mindset and mentality can be adopted to help you face the trial that has landed on your doorstep, no matter what it is. And, thankfully, while cancer and other challenges are not contagious, optimism is. When you adopt a positive, upbeat attitude, the friends and family surrounding you will follow suit. This synergy will result in a manifested environment of happiness and optimism, full of people who are moving confidently into the future, carrying with them all the lessons of the past.

Optimism is a choice. You can choose to live the way I have, putting into practice the unwavering optimistic attitude that has become my signature in every area of my life. We are our best selves because of the relationships and examples of the incredible people we are blessed to have and learn from in our lives. In all circumstance, stay on the B course:

Be a warrior.
Be rocket fuel to the communities you serve.
Be a blessing to yourself and others.
Be courageous.
Most of all, be faithful!

I know what it is to suffer, and as near impossible as it was—and continues to be—I am grateful for the woman I became thanks to the road I have traveled and the one I keep moving forward on.

Thank you so much for purchasing this book, together we are raising money for cancer research. All proceeds from this book will continue to fund these life-saving efforts and resources.

Wishing you abundant blessings, joy, love, and optimism,

Kimmie

ALL BOOK ROYALTIES ARE BEING DONATED TO A PREMIER ACADEMIC RESEARCH INSTITUTION FOR INTEGRATED BREAST CANCER FUND AND PATIENT CARE, AND AMERICAN CANCER SOCIETY ASTRAZENECA HOPE LODGE IN PHILADELPHIA, PENNSYLVANIA

REFERENCES

Brody, Jane E. "A Positive Outlook May Be Good for Your Health." *The New York Times*. March 27, 2017. Accessed September 23, 2020. www.nytimes.com/2017/03/27/well/live/positive-thinking-may-improve-health-and-extend-life.html.

DebtConsolidation.com. "How Tyler Perry Went From Homeless To A Net Worth of $400 Million." Debt Consolidation Team. Last updated February 5, 2019. Accessed September 23, 2020. www.debtconsolidation.com/tyler-perry/.

DiSalvo, David. "Six Science-Based Reasons Why Laughter Is The Best Medicine." *Forbes*. June 5, 2017. Accessed September 23, 2020. www.forbes.com/sites/daviddisalvo/2017/06/05/six-science-based-reasons-why-laughter-is-the-best-medicine/#306a2b117f04.

Fang, Ruolian, Blaine Landis, Zhen Zhang, Marc H. Anderson, Jason D. Shaw, and Martin Kilduff. "Integrating Personality and Social Networks: A Meta-Analysis of Personality, Network Position, and Work Outcomes in Organizations." *Organization Science* 26, no. 4 (July 2015): 941–1261. doi.org/10.1287/orsc.2015.0972.

Fruen, Lauren. "Body of Autistic Boy, 9, 'Twice Pushed into Florida Canal by His Mother Had Signs of Head Trauma' After He Was Drowned 'In a Fake Abduction Plot'." *Daily Mail*. Updated May 26, 2020. Accessed September 23, 2020. www.dailymail.co.uk/news/article-8359233/Body-autistic-boy-9-twice-pushed-Florida-canal-mother-signs-head-trauma.html.

Goleman, Daniel. "'Social Chameleon' May Pay Emotional Price." *The New York Times*. March 12, 1985. Accessed September 23, 2020. www.nytimes.com/1985/03/12/science/social-chameleon-may-pay-emotional-price.html.

Groth, Aimee. "You're the Average of the Five People You Spend the Most Time With." *Business Insider*. July 24, 2012. Accessed September 23, 2020. www.businessinsider.com/jim-rohn-youre-the-average-of-the-five-people-you-spend-the-most-time-with-2012-7.

Haseman, Janie, Karina Zaiets, Mitchell Thorson, Carlie Procell, George Petras, and Shawn J. Sullivan. "Tracking Protests Across the USA in the Wake of George Floyd's Death." *USA Today*. June 18, 2020. Accessed September 23, 2020. www.usatoday.com/in-depth/graphics/2020/06/03/map-protests-wake-george-floyds-death/5310149002/.

The Help SAVE Foundation. "Domestic Violence Statistics." Accessed September 23, 2020. www.thehelpsavefoundation.org/about-us/domestic-violence-statistics/.

Mackay, Harvey. "Optimists See Opportunities in Challenges." *Harvey Mackay* blog. May 25, 2017. Accessed September 23, 2020. harveymackay.com/optimists-see-opportunities-in-challenges/.

Marriage Builders. "The Love Bank." Accessed September 23, 2020. www.marriagebuilders.com/the-love-bank.htm.

Mayo Clinic Health System. "Helping People, Changing Lives: The 6 Health Benefits of Volunteering." May 18, 2017. Accessed September 23, 2020. www.mayoclinichealthsystem.org/hometown-health/speaking-of-health/helping-people-changing-lives-the-6-health-benefits-of-volunteering.

Morin, Amy. "5 Reasons You Have to Accept Pain If You Want to Be Happy." *Psychology Today*. November 14, 2015. Accessed September 23, 2020. www.psychologytoday.com/us/blog/what-mentally-strong-people-dont-do/201511/5-reasons-you-have-accept-pain-if-you-want-be-happy.

Palmiotto, Jenny. "The Power of Positivity." Family Guidance and Therapy blog. July 11, 2013. Accessed September 23, 2020. familyguidanceandtherapy.com/the-power-of-positivity/.

Piferi, Rachel L., and Kathleen A. Lawler. "Social Support and Ambulatory Blood Pressure: An Examination of Both Receiving and Giving." *International Journal of Psychophysiology* 62, no. 2 (November 2006): 328–336. doi.org/10.1016/j.ijpsycho.2006.06.002.

Poulin, Michael J., Stephanie L. Brown, Amanda J. Dillard, and Dylan M. Smith. "Giving to Others and the Association Between Stress and Mortality." *American Journal of Public Health* 103, no. 9 (September 2013): 1649–1645. doi: 10.2105/AJPH.2012.300876

Psychology Today. "Mindfulness: Present Moment Awareness." Accessed September 23, 2020. www.psychologytoday.com/us/basics/mindfulness.

Psychology Today. "Perfectionism." Accessed September 23, 2020. www.psychologytoday.com/us/basics/perfectionism.

Razzetti, Gustavo. "The Bright and Dark Sides of Pessimism." *The Ladders* news. January 30, 2019. Accessed September 23, 2020. www.theladders.com/career-advice/the-bright-and-dark-sides-of-optimism-and-pessimism.

Russian, Ale. "Tyler Perry's Billionaire Status Is Official on Latest Forbes List." *People*. September 2, 2020. Accessed September 23, 2020. people.com/movies/tyler-perrys-billionaire-status-is-official-on-latest-forbes-list/.

S., Pangambam. "The Power of Vulnerability by Brene Brown (Transcript)." *The Singju Post.* September 5, 2014. Accessed September 23, 2020. singjupost. com/power-vulnerability-brene-brown-transcript/?print=print.

Souza, Eduardo. "How Lighting Affects Mood." Arch Daily. August 12, 2019. Accessed September 23, 2020. www.archdaily.com/922506/how-lighting -affects-mood.

Susan G. Komen. "Breast Cancer Statistics." Last updated May 18, 2020. Accessed September 23, 2020. ww5.komen.org/BreastCancer/Statistics.html.

Sylvester, Brad. "Fact Check: Did Churchill Say, 'An Optimist Sees The Opportunity in Every Difficulty'?" Check Your Fact. July 25, 2019. Accessed September 23, 2020. checkyourfact.com/2019/07/25/fact-check-winston-churchill -optimist-opportunity-every-difficulty/.

University of Maryland Medical Center. "Laughter Helps Blood Vessels Function Better." Science Daily. March 16, 2005. Accessed September 23, 2020. www.sciencedaily.com/releases/2005/03/050310100458.htm.

Valley Heart Institute. "Women & Heart Disease: 20 Fast Facts About Women and Heart Disease." Accessed September 23, 2020. valleyheartinstitute. com/cardiovascular-services/women-heart-disease/.

Winch, PhD, Guy. *Emotional First Aid: Healing Rejection, Guilt, Failure, and Other Everyday Hurts.* New York, NY: Hudson Street Press, 2013.

ABOUT KIMBERLY S. REED,
DIVERSITY, EQUALITY, AND INCLUSION STRATEGIST

KIMBERLY S. REED is an award-winning international speaker, author, corporate trainer, and diversity, equality and inclusion executive, and a nationally recognized thought leader. She is an expert strategist and advisor to some of the world's most influential organizations in global professional services, health care, financial services, consumer products, and pharmaceutical industries. A seasoned leader in transforming organizations into high-performing enterprises and challenging leaders to live without limits, she has more than twenty years of human resources, talent acquisition, and diversity and inclusion experience, and has successfully turned around troubled diversity practices by designing, building, leading, and shaping high-performing cultures at global organizations with robust strategies, global employee development programs, and enterprise-wide initiatives that have increased revenue growth and organizational brand eminence.

For more information, visit *www.thereeddevelopmentgroup.com.*